Facilitator's notes

D1824985

Introduction

Information for managers
Length of workshop 4 hours, including a break
Facilitation skills This workshop requires presentation skills and the management of facilitated discussion and small-group activities. The facilitator must have experience of mainstreaming gender equality in development, humanitarian, or advocacy programmes, or in an NGO as an organisation. Managers are responsible for ensuring that this workshop is delivered by a suitable member of staff.
Learners This workshop is intended for all staff who need to understand the importance of working on gender equality.
Preparation by learners None.
Size of group This course could be run for groups of 3–20. However, it is easier for learners to ask questions, and easier for facilitators to manage the activities, if groups consist of 6–12 participants.

Information for facilitators
Room This workshop requires space for the whole group to work together in a room, sitting in such a way that they can all see one another. It also requires sufficient space for the group to divide into smaller groups of about five persons.
Equipment needed ▪ Flipchart stand, pens, and paper. ▪ Laptop and data projector, or an overhead projector (using pre-printed acetate slides). ▪ Cards (big enough for the writing on them to be legible when the cards are posted on the wall). ▪ Some means of attaching paper and cards to the wall, e.g. Blutack, pins, or sticky tape.

Preparation of material
1. Photocopy the agenda and the handouts:
 	
    ▪ Handout 1: 'Gender glossary' (for Session 2)
    ▪ Handout 2: 'Statements for ranking' (for Session 3)
    ▪ Handout 3: 'Mathare case study' (print this out as a handout for Session 4)
    ▪ Handout 4: 'Oxfam GB's policy on gender equality' (for Session 5)
    ▪ Handout 5: 'Evaluation form' (for Session 6)

2. Copy the PowerPoint slides (pages 42–61) and the slides for Handout 3 (pages 26–32) (or from the PowerPoint files on the CD) on to acetate slides (unless you are using a data projector).

3. Write the agenda for the day on a flipchart sheet and put it up on the wall where all participants can see it. Use this to guide them through the day; make any changes to the timings if they become necessary.

Supplementary information

These documents provide background information to help you to support the participants. They are not intended for use as lecturing material or to hand out to participants. (You are a facilitator, not a lecturer.) However, if you think the briefs would be particularly useful to the learners and the learners would have time to read them, they could be photocopied and distributed.

*   'How does poverty relate to gender inequality?' (for Session 3): this gives many examples of gender inequality and the ways in which poverty is experienced differently by women and by men. It also provides some basic ideas about ways in which an NGO like Oxfam can respond to inequality.
*   'Oxfam GB's rationale for work on gender equality' (for Sessions 4 and 5). If you read nothing else, read this.

Linked learning

Books:
*   *The Oxfam Gender Training Manual*, Suzanne Williams with Janet Seed and Adelina Mwau, Oxfam GB, 1995.
*   *A Guide to Gender-Analysis Frameworks*, Candida March, Ines Smyth, and Maitrayee Mukhopadhyay, Oxfam GB, 1999.
*   *Gender Works: Oxfam Experience in Policy and Practice*, Fenella Porter, Ines Smyth, and Caroline Sweetman (eds.), Oxfam GB, 1999.
*   *Gender Equality and Men: Learning from Practice*, Sandy Ruxton (ed.), Oxfam GB, 2004.

Internet:
*   www.undp.org/gender/ Contains UNDP gender-mainstreaming information and tools.
*   www.unifem.org News and resources on gender and development issues.
*   www.worldbank.org/gender/ The GenderNet provides experience-based information about gender and development.

People:
*   For Oxfam staff, expert support is available within Oxfam GB from Regional Gender Advisers, the Programme Policy Team, and the Humanitarian Department Gender Adviser.

Translations

This module is currently available in English, Spanish, French, and Portuguese. If it would help learners, please feel free to translate all or part of it into additional languages, but please send a copy to the Oxfam Publishing Team at Oxfam House in Oxford (address at the front of this pack).

Support and feedback

*   Please send questions, ideas, and feedback to learninternational@oxfam.org.uk

Workshop objectives

During the workshop, participants will:

Know …
Understand the relationship between gender inequality and poverty, and why Oxfam needs to promote gender equality.

Feel …
Motivated to challenge gender-based discrimination, and mobilised to find out more about how to do this and how to act.

Do …
Attempt a basic gender analysis, using a case study.
As a result of this workshop, participants will understand that Oxfam is concerned to address the injustice faced by poor women throughout the world, and to challenge the abuse of their rights. They will understand why Oxfam believes that it cannot effectively and sustainably alleviate poverty without addressing related gender inequality.

This is a basic workshop for use with all kinds of staff, but it can be adapted to meet the precise requirements of particular participants.

Optional pre-course questionnaire

You may find it helpful to acquire information in advance about the participants' expectations and current levels of knowledge. You could do this by asking the questions below, either face to face or by telephone.

1. Have you attended any other gender-equality training course?
2. What do you hope to learn from this workshop?
3. What are the main gender-related issues that you encounter in your work?

Asking such questions will also help you to establish a trusting relationship with individual participants on a sometimes sensitive subject.

Case study

One case study is provided as a basis for this workshop. It has been carefully designed to be relevant in most geographical contexts. If you feel that it would make your workshops more effective, you could replace it with a more relevant text, but you should use the following criteria when choosing one.

1. It should include clear examples of the relationship between poverty and gender inequality.
2. It should be no longer than one page in length, or six PowerPoint slides.

Timetable

Start	Finish	Session
0000	0045	1. Introductions and energiser
0045	0115	2. Basic concepts of gender
0115	0215	3. Gender inequality and poverty
0215	0230	BREAK
0230	0330	4. Why working on gender inequality is important
0330	0345	5. Oxfam GB's policy on gender equality
0345	0400	6. Course evaluation

The timings for this four-hour event are shown as starting from 00.00. The actual start-time will depend on the group's normal working hours.

Note to facilitator

The subject of gender usually stimulates many questions and debates. Much useful learning can come out of such discussions, but it is important to move the course along and delay questions until the relevant part of the course – when they may be covered anyway.

- Pay careful attention to the timings of the workshop and chair the sessions strictly. Explain to the participants that not every question can be asked or answered in the time allowed.

- Put up a page of flipchart paper on the wall and use it to 'park' questions that cannot be answered immediately. This is a way of acknowledging the question. Explain how answers will be provided: for example, by referring questions to an appropriate colleague.

- In order to maintain the pace of the course, it is important to provide clear instructions and information about timings. Five minutes before the end of each group exercise, tell the learners that five minutes remain; one minute before the end, tell them that they have one more minute. Always finish the session on time. Groups working under pressure tend to produce better results.

- During group work, circulate among the groups to make sure that they have understood the exercise and are working effectively.

Session 1

Introductions and energiser

TOTAL TIME:
45 minutes

Purpose: to introduce the facilitator and participants to each other, to present the goals of the workshop, and to help participants to understand Oxfam's aim in terms of gender equality.

Timing	What YOU do	What the LEARNERS do	Resources
00.00	▪ Welcome everyone, introduce yourself, show Slide 1. ▪ Ask the participants to introduce themselves briefly, stating their names, their roles, and their reasons for attending this workshop. ▪ Ask them to reflect in pairs for five minutes on their ideal vision of gender equality. ▪ Ask each pair to draw a picture that expresses this vision of gender equality. It may take any form, including a diagram or a cartoon, provided that it is a picture that they can use to explain their vision. After five minutes, put the pictures up at the front of the room and ask one person from each pair to explain what the image means. ▪ Note down on a flipchart the concepts that emerge from what they say.	▪ Introduce themselves, giving their name, their role, their reason for being here. ▪ In pairs discuss their vision of gender equality and draw a picture to represent it.	**Slide 1** Flipchart paper and pens
00.30	• Present the objectives for this workshop, using Slide 2. • Go through the day's agenda, which you have written on a flipchart sheet. • Show the suggested ground rules, using Slide 3. • Ask for comments and suggestions.	• Check that they agree with each of these, and express any concerns and suggestions.	**Slides 2 and 3:** Objectives and suggested ground rules
00.45			

Session 2

Basic concepts of gender

TOTAL TIME: 30 minutes

Purpose: to demystify the concept of gender and the main related issues, and reassure participants that these are simple ideas to which they can easily relate.

Timing	What YOU do	What the LEARNERS do	Resources
00.45	• Ask participants to call out definitions of the terms *sex* and *gender*. Take a few answers. Then say that the group will now consider how Oxfam defines those terms. This could start a very big debate. Your role is to encourage everyone to contribute, without wasting a lot of time.	• Identify the concepts that they feel require clear definitions.	**Slides 4, 5, 6, 7** on sex and gender, gender-equality mainstreaming, and practical and strategic needs.
	• Show them Slides 4, 5, and 6. Introduce the concept of gender-equality mainstreaming in development and humanitarian work, and explain that it is about applying a gender-sensitive approach to all policies and programmes.	• Develop definitions for terms that they feel to be in greatest need of clarification.	
	• Show Slide 7 on strategic and practical needs, explaining the difference.		
	• Ask them to brainstorm any gender-related terms in common usage in their work contexts that in their opinion need clearer definition.		
	• List these on a flipchart.		
	• Identify the main ones, and ask participants to form pairs to try to define them.		
	• Then give out Handout 1 to confirm how Oxfam chooses to define most of the gender-related terms that are in common use.		**Handout 1:** 'Gender glossary'.
	• Clarify any common confusions, such as whether people actually mean sex-disaggregated data when they say 'gender-disaggregated data'.		
01.15	• Park any terms for which adequate definitions have not been identified. Arrange to refer these to a Gender Adviser for an explanation.		

Session 3   Gender inequality and poverty

2 pages   **TOTAL TIME:** 1 hour

Purpose: to motivate participants to want to address gender-based injustice in the world.

Timing	What YOU do	What the LEARNERS do	Resources
01.15	• Ask each participant take five minutes to think of the example of gender inequality that most angers them. • Then give them five minutes to express this as a picture, a cartoon, or a diagram, or in writing. • Provide them with cards, paper, and felt-tip pens. • At the end of the ten minutes, ask them to place their ideas up on the wall where they can be seen by all. But avoid entering into discussions about any particular issue at this point.	• Describe the example of gender inequality that most angers them; express this either visually or in words.	Paper Cards Felt-tip pens
01.30	• Show Slides 8–19. As you go through the quiz questions, ask participants to call out their answers. Once you know what people in the group think, then tell them the answers. • Discuss any surprises for the group arising from the answer slides.	• Think about quiz questions, offer answers, and check their answers. • Discuss any surprising results.	**Slides 8–19:** Key facts on gender inequality; and a quiz

Timing	What YOU do	What the LEARNERS do	Resources
1.45	**Statement-ranking activity** • Ask the group to form pairs. Tell them that they will be asked to look at a series of statements and to decide if they agree or disagree with them. • Ask the pairs to choose the statement that they most strongly agree with (ranking it first) and the statement that they most strongly disagree with (ranking it ninth). • Give out Handout 2. • Explain that there are no right or wrong answers. The point of the exercise is to get them to engage with some of the major gender-inequality aspects of women's economic roles.	• Decide in pairs which statements they most strongly agree with and which they most strongly disagree with, negotiating their opinions with their partners, influencing and listening, as they feel appropriate.	**Handout 2**: 'Statements for ranking'
2.15	• Once they have agreed on the two statements, explain that this is the end of the exercise.		

02.15-02.30	BREAK

Remember that a break is an important aspect of learning. Encourage the group to get up and walk around, but ask them not to get involved in other work, such as making telephone calls.

Session 4 Why working on gender inequality is important 2 pages TOTAL TIME: 1 hour

Purpose: to motivate staff to participate actively in Oxfam's work to address gender injustice.

Timing	What YOU do	What the LEARNERS do	Resources
02.30	• Ask the participants if they think it is important to work on gender inequality within their programme, and if so why. You should bring out the following points: o that NGOs like Oxfam are concerned to address the injustice of gender inequality and the world-wide abuse of poor women's rights; o that we recognise that we cannot alleviate poverty without addressing related gender inequality. • Show the PowerPoint slides about the Kenya Mathare case study, which you have also printed out as Handout 3. Organise participants in groups of four or five people to consider the information provided. • Ask them to discuss the main ways in which poverty in Mathare is related to gender inequality and the lack of women's rights. Which issues would need to be addressed in order to alleviate poverty? • Ask them to agree on the three most important issues, and report their decision to a plenary session, writing each point on a card or post-it note. • Stick the cards or post-its up on the wall, organising them by themes: for example, the economy, education, health, political issues. There are no fixed correct answers, but answers might include the following: 1. Women have less access to land. 2. Women earn less than men. 3. Women are more dependent on social services than men because of their child-caring activities, which make it more difficult for them to engage in paid work. 4. The pollution of water and the environment affects women more, because	• Form groups and consider the Kenya Mathare Case Study, discussing how poverty and gender inequality are linked in this location.	**Slides:** Mathare case study **Handout 3:** The Mathare slides, Cards or post-its

Timing	What YOU do	What the LEARNERS do	Resources
	4. The pollution of water and the environment affects women more, because of their domestic and child-caring responsibilities.		
	5. Women are less well educated than men and have fewer vocational opportunities.		
	6. Women are more vulnerable to HIV/AIDS.		
	7. Young girls marry very young, which makes it more difficult for them to earn a living and provide for their children.		
03.30	• Explain that in this session they have carried out the first stage in mainstreaming gender equality, which is to recognise the different impacts of poverty on women and men.		

Session 5   Oxfam GB policy on gender equality

TOTAL TIME:
15 minutes

Purpose : to ensure that participants understand the policy and its relevance for their work.

Timing	What YOU do	What the LEARNERS do	Resources
03.30	• Show Slide 20. • Give participants Handout 4.	• Consider Oxfam GB's gender policy and discuss how it relates to their own work. How can they improve the way in which they implement the policy?	**Slide 20**: 'Gender Policy' **Handout 4**: 'Oxfam GB policy on gender equality'
03.45	• Ask participants to read the handout, and then discuss in pairs how they can improve their implementation of this policy within their own functions and roles.		

Session 6

Course evaluation

TOTAL TIME: 15 minutes

Purpose : to think about how this course will be used in the workplace, and to evaluate the workshop.

Timing	What YOU do	What the LEARNERS do	Resources

03.45	• Ask participants to describe:
	   ○ one thing that they will do differently in their work as a result of participating in this workshop, and
	   ○ one aspect of the course that could be improved.
	• Ask them to complete the evaluation form (Handout 5) before leaving the room.
	• Discuss whether any of the products of the workshop could be used for future action planning, such as efforts to mainstream gender equality.
		• Evaluate what they have learned from the workshop, comment on any improvements needed, and think about how they will use the workshop to take forward work on gender equality.	**Handout 5**: 'Evaluation form'

4.00			

Handout 1: Gender glossary

GAD (gender and development)	An approach which addresses inequalities in the social roles of women and men, in relation to development.
GDI (Gender Development Index)	A tool for comparing women's and men's life expectancies, educational attainments, and incomes.
gender	A concept which refers to the comparative or differential roles, responsibilities, and opportunities (all socially constructed) of women and men in a given society.
gender analysis	An approach which explores the inequalities in the relations between women and men in a given society (as well as the inequalities between women according to age, class, etc.), and assesses the disadvantages that women themselves identify as a cause for concern.In this approach, data are separated ('disaggregated') by sex, and the ways in which labour, roles, needs, and participation are divided and valued according to sex are examined.
gender balance	The participation of an equal number of women and men within an activity or organisation, such as representation on committees or in decision-making structures.
gender equality	Identical treatment of women and men in laws and policies, and access to resources and services.
gender equity	A broader term, indicating general fairness of treatment for women and men, according to their respective needs.
gender-equality mainstreaming	A process of ensuring that all policy, programme, administrative, and financial activities contribute to gender equality, by transforming the balance of power between women and men.
gender relations	Ways in which power, rights, roles, responsibilities, and identities are ascribed to women and men in relation to each other.
gender-sensitive	Recognising differences and inequities between female and male needs, roles, responsibilities, and identities.
gender-specific	Targeted only at the needs and interests of either women/girls or men/boys as special categories, within existing gender divisions.
sex-disaggregated data	Information presented according to numbers of males and females in a given population.
gender-disaggregated data	Data collected about males and females separately in relation to all aspects of their functioning – ethnicity, class, caste, age, location, etc.
gender indicator	A marker to measure gender-related changes, e.g. in terms of improved gender equality.
sex	The biological difference between men and women: not dependent on culture
Women in Development	An approach which includes women in development projects in order to make the projects more efficient.

Handout 2: Statements for ranking (for Session 3)

WOMEN HAVE CHILDREN	WOMEN DO IT ALL	WOMEN NEED NEW SKILLS
Women don't need to be financially independent of men, because all they do is have children and get married.	Women are financially worse off than men because men are lazy and don't do any of the housework or child care, so women have to do it all and they don't get paid for this work.	To improve their economic position, women need help to develop the skills necessary to obtain paid work.
ONE'S OWN DECISION	WOMEN HAVE SKILLS	MEN WON'T CHANGE
It is for women themselves to decide what they want to do. It is not for other people, like the government, to interfere. Anyway, there is nothing wrong with being a housewife or a mother.	Women have many skills and abilities which they learn while running a home, but these are not recognised by employers when women apply for paid work.	Women are economically worse off than men because men won't change. Men are worried that change will mean that they lose out. If men won't change, then it's up to women to change things for themselves.
WOMEN SHOULDN'T WORK	WOMEN DO UNPAID WORK	WOMEN NEED LAWS FOR EQUALITY
In a time of high unemployment, women should not expect to go out to work. It's better if they stay at home and look after the children, so there are enough jobs for men.	Women are economically worse off than men because society does not take responsibility for child care and looking after old people and disabled people, but expects women to do these things without pay.	Women are economically worse off than men because governments are not interested in passing laws to promote equality.

Handout 3: Mathare case study

Handout 3 is a set of PowerPoint slides, presented as a separate file on the Pick-up-and-Go CD.

The facilitator should copy pages 26–32 as a handout for each participant, in addition to showing it as PowerPoint slides.

Pick-up-and-Go Training Pack • Introduction to Gender Equality: Handout 3

Land Rights in
Mathare Slum, Nairobi, Kenya

This material is used with kind permission of Esther Mwaura Muriu of GrootsKenya.

Handout 3: Slide 1

PICK–UP–AND–GO

Pick-up-and-Go Training Pack • Introduction to Gender Equality: Handout 3

Land access in Kenya

❖ Land rights and land ownership have been a major problem in Kenya since the time of Independence.

❖ This is especially so in urban areas. By 2007, it is expected that more than 50 per cent of the world's population will live in urban areas, placing more pressure on land-tenure systems.

❖ More than 25 per cent of the urban people in Kenya live in absolute poverty and have no access to land.

❖ The HIV/AIDS epidemic is currently making things worse, affecting mainly young and middle-aged groups.

PICK-UP-AND-GO

Mathare

- Mathare, about 5 km east of Nairobi, Kenya's capital, is one of Africa's largest and worst slums. The population of half a million is increasing as rural people migrate to Nairobi in search of work.

- It consists of a maze of shacks with rusty iron-sheeting roofs, mud walls, and open sewage gutters.

- Population density is high:1,200 people per hectare.

- More than 70 per cent of the inhabitants earn less than one dollar a day, on average.

- The slum has inadequate basic services.

- There is no more land in Mathare for allocation or distribution. Most is in the hands of private developers.

PICK–UP–AND–GO

Living conditions in Mathare

- Environmental problems – garbage and human waste, broken sewers, lack of clean water, poor housing.

PICK−UP−AND−GO

Survival strategies in Mathare

- Domestic work, washing clothes.
- Selling illicitly brewed beer, traditional medicines, maize, beans, etc.
- Recycling garbage.
- Tailoring.
- Labouring in the fields along Nairobi River.
- Carpentry.
- Working as carers for HIV/AIDS patients.

PICK–UP–AND–GO

Women in Mathare

- Few women have completed basic formal school or have received any significant technical training.

- Girls marry young, generally between the ages of 13 and 20.

- It is common for women's property to be seized by their ex-husbands or their deceased husbands' families. As a result, destitute women move into the city from the rural areas. More and more men are dying of AIDS, so the problem is getting worse.

Handout 3: Slide 6

PICK–UP–AND–GO

Group exercise

- Consider the information provided.

- Identify and imagine the main ways in which poverty is related to gender inequality and the lack of women's rights in Mathare.

- Agree the three most important aspects and write these on cards ready for the plenary session.

PICK–UP–AND–GO

Handout 4: Oxfam GB policy on gender equality

(for Session 5; 2 pages)

Oxfam's mission is to work with others to overcome poverty and suffering.

People experience poverty when they are denied the right to livelihoods, water, education and health, protection and security, a voice in public life, or freedom from discrimination. Oxfam's definition of poverty goes beyond the purely economic to encompass capabilities, powerlessness, and inequality.

Women often have less recourse than men to legal recognition and protection, as well as lower access to public knowledge and information, and less decision-making power both within and outside the home. Women in many parts of the world frequently have little control over fertility, sexuality, and marital choices. This systematic discrimination reduces women's public participation, often increases their vulnerability to poverty, violence, and HIV, and results in women representing a disproportionate percentage of the poor population of the world.

Gender equality gives women and men the same entitlements to all aspects of human development, including economic, social, cultural, civil, and political rights; the same level of respect; the same opportunities to make choices; and the same level of power to shape the outcomes of these choices. [1]

This policy represents our organisational commitment to gender equality. It has been written to help staff and volunteers ensure that our work improves the lives of both women and men and promotes gender equality.

Principles

- Throughout the organisation, we will base our work on a common understanding that gender equality is key to overcoming poverty and suffering.

- We will work with both women and men to address the specific ideas and beliefs that create and reinforce gender-related poverty.

- Women and girls will be empowered through all aspects of our programme and ways of working, and we will often prioritise work which specifically raises the status of women.

- Our own internal practices, and ways of working, will reflect our commitment to gender equality.

Strategies for achieving gender equality

- A thorough understanding of the different concerns, experiences, capacities, and needs of women and men will shape the way in which we analyse, plan, implement, and evaluate all our work.

---

1 Adapted from Marsha Freeman, Oxfam GB Gender Review, September 2001.

- We will address the policies, practices, ideas, and beliefs that perpetuate gender inequality and prevent women and girls (and sometimes men and boys) from enjoying a decent livelihood, participation in public life, protection, and basic services.

- We will seek to ensure the full participation and empowerment of women in all areas of our work, and will promote women's rights as human rights, particularly in the areas of abuse and violence.

- We will work with both men and women, together and separately, to have a more lasting impact on beliefs and behaviour. We will ensure that any work that we do with men and men's groups supports the promotion of gender equality.

- Partnerships and alliances will be assessed on the basis of their commitment to gender equality.

- Our campaign, advocacy, and media messages, and the images that we use to support these, will emphasise the importance of gender equality in overcoming poverty and suffering. Our communications will also highlight our own commitment to gender equality, and the essential role played by women in all aspects of development and humanitarian work.

- Managers will encourage groups and forums across the organisation to share learning and best practice on gender equality. Gender training will also be made available to staff and volunteers.

- In all our work we will demonstrate commitment to gender equality through setting appropriate team and individual objectives, and through allocating adequate staff and resources to enable us to fulfil the gender-equality policy.

- Managers of all divisions will devise and report on measurable objectives and actions relating to the gender-equality policy; and our management, finance, and human-resource systems will facilitate and contribute to our gender work.

- Gender awareness and understanding will be used as a criterion for recruitment and development of staff and volunteers.

- Within the organisation we will pursue family-friendly work practices that enable both men and women to participate fully in work and family life.

This gender policy is closely linked to Oxfam GB's Equal Opportunities and Diversity Policies.

Handout 5: Course evaluation (for Session 6)

Name (optional): _____ **Date:** _____

For each question where there is a scale, please circle the relevant number.

1. **I understand the basic concepts related to gender.**

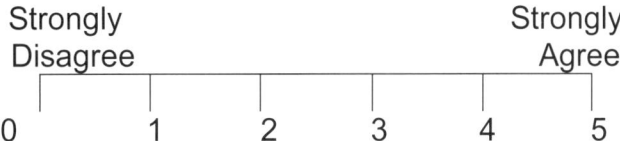

2. **I understand the relevance of addressing gender inequality in the struggle against poverty and for human rights.**

3. **I understand why it is important to address gender inequality in our programmes and ways of working.**

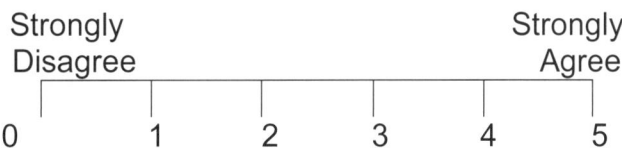

Is there anything that could be done differently to improve any of the scores that you have given?
How could the facilitator improve his or her skills in helping others to learn?

Thank you for taking the time to fill out this course evaluation.

Supplementary information (1)
How does poverty relate to gender inequality?
(for Session 3)

(Note: this is not a handout)

All the governments participating in the UN Fourth World Conference on Women agreed on a useful definition of poverty:

Poverty has various manifestations, including lack of food and productive resources sufficient to ensure a sustainable livelihood; hunger and malnutrition; ill health; limited or lack of access to education and other basic services; increasing morbidity and mortality from illness; homelessness and inadequate housing; unsafe environments; and social discrimination and exclusion. It is also characterised by lack of participation in decision-making and in civil, social and political life. It occurs in all countries – as mass poverty in many developing countries and as pockets of poverty in developed countries (Beijing Platform of Action, United Nations, 1996).

Both women and men living in poverty would recognise the key elements on this list. But gender inequality means that women's experience of poverty differs from men's experience of poverty, and therefore the solutions are different in each case.

Do poor women outnumber poor men?

Yes. It is impossible to quote precise figures, but most observers agree that the imbalance is getting worse. We often hear the statement, 'Women are 70 per cent of the world's poor'; but some statisticians say that the proportion is closer to 55 or 60 per cent. However, all agree that the degree of women's poverty is worsening.

Current ways of measuring poverty fail to identify gender-related differences, for several reasons:

- Poverty statistics usually focus on households, not individuals, so they don't identify unequal treatment within a family. However, female-headed households *can* be counted, and it is clear that most (though not all) are economically poorer than households headed by men.
- Measurements of poverty focus only on economic want – not on powerlessness, violence and abuse, and the exhaustion caused by women's heavy and often unequal workloads. All these are essential aspects of poverty as Oxfam understands it.
- Poverty measurements give us a single 'snapshot' of household poverty at a particular time. They don't capture changes over time. Women's livelihoods tend to be less secure than men's, so women and their dependants are vulnerable to sudden crises and repeated periods of impoverishment.
- Official economic analysis focuses only on production undertaken for cash. It ignores production for household consumption, and all the unpaid work of caring for family and household. This leads to inappropriate and unfair economic policies which ignore the great contribution that women make to development; such policies further reinforce gender inequality.

Is poverty 'different' for women and men?

Yes. To return to the UN's definition of poverty, given above:

- *lack of food... hunger and malnutrition:* women and girls are often expected to eat the leftovers after the men and boys have finished eating.

- *lack of productive resources sufficient to ensure a sustainable livelihood:* most women do not have legal or traditional rights to land or other assets. They can't get loans or credit, because they have no collateral. Other resources needed for success in business include skills training, time, and information about markets. Women are less likely to have these resources than men, and hence they are concentrated in low-return, insecure, informal occupations. Lacking alternatives, many cannot leave abusive men, because they are wholly dependent on them for their survival.

- *ill health... increasing morbidity and mortality from illness:* in countries where people pay for health care, women are less likely than men to seek treatment in hospitals or clinics when they are ill, and more likely either to treat themselves at home or consult traditional healers. Pregnancy and childbearing carry heavy risks for women who lack access to trained support. Women are also more likely than men to look after sick family members.

- *limited or lack of access to education and other basic services:* two-thirds of the children who don't attend school are girls. Many of them are kept at home, doing housework and looking after other children. Some girl children are already married. Parents may decide not to send girls to school because of fears for their physical safety on the journey there – and even at school, where male teachers and pupils may sexually molest them.

- *homelessness and inadequate housing:* if a marriage breaks down, or a daughter displeases her parents, in most societies it is the woman who has to leave her home, because she has no rights of ownership – regardless of the contribution that she has made to the family. Women-headed households are more likely to live in sub-standard housing.

- *unsafe environments:* gender-based violence, including rape, makes it dangerous for women in all societies to move around outside their homes. Home is often not a safe place either, since domestic violence is widespread, and often condoned by society. If war breaks out, adult men are the first to be called to fight, while women and children are more likely to suffer as civilian casualties. Men traditionally do risky work, like mining or fire-fighting, but increasingly women are also working with unsafe chemicals and technologies, in both factories and fields.

- *social discrimination and exclusion...lack of participation in decision making and in civil, social, and political life:* poor men are excluded from government because they are poor. Poor women are excluded for two reasons: poverty and gender. In most societies, women are grossly under-represented in government. No parliament in the world has equal representation of women and men. In many societies, women are also excluded from or under-represented in local decision-making bodies. Economic and financial policies are developed without recognising women's economic contributions in the unpaid and informal parts of the economy.

What can an NGO like Oxfam do about all this?

Gender equality is an essential part of poverty alleviation. Sometimes this recognition has led to development projects that focus on female-headed households. Households headed by women often lack representation on local decision-making bodies that distribute resources. Women heads of household may not even be allowed to do essential things, like ploughing land, because of cultural taboos. Development projects may focus on raising the income of women-headed households, and supporting such women to gain a voice in the community.

But working to alleviate the poverty of women in general is not enough. There is good evidence that if gender inequality exists *within* a household, that household is more likely to continue to be poor. Two-thirds of households worldwide are headed by men. So without promoting equality for women in these households, it is impossible to alleviate poverty for the majority in any community. Projects working with women in male-headed households tend to focus on increasing women's participation in community-level decision making, and promoting their role in production. Such projects also need to promote gender equality inside the household.

How does gender equality benefit poor families headed by men?

*   Evidence from both developing and developed countries demonstrates that women are more altruistic than men in the way they choose to spend household income. The greater women's control of family budgets, the better the nutritional status and health of the whole family.
*   Some evidence suggests that if a woman is educated, her family is likely to be smaller. Smaller family size usually correlates with less poverty.
*   Women and men can maximise their livelihood opportunities by doing whatever work is most useful, regardless of restrictive assumptions about men's and women's roles.

Overall, if all family members, including women, are permitted to combine their skills and knowledge to make genuinely joint decisions on livelihoods and family size, the family is more likely to stay together, survive poverty, and move on to better times.

What might NGOs like Oxfam do to help?

Development projects that aim to alleviate poverty need to mainstream gender equality throughout all their activities, with measures that include the following:

*   Raising awareness about gender and poverty, and supporting women and men in livelihoods activities which are appropriate for them as individual members of families, rather than as 'women' or 'men'.
*   Challenging violence against women at home and in the community.
*   Supporting women who are abused at home.
*   Supporting men to end violence against women, inside and outside the home.
*   Challenging conventional assumptions about gender which prevent women and men maximising their skills in the marketplace. (Why shouldn't women go to market? Shouldn't men help out at home?)
*   Educating both women and men about family planning.

Finally, development organisations need to support women to challenge unfair, inappropriate economic and social policies which make life harder for women.

Caroline Sweetman, Oxfam GB Campaigns and Policy Department
(with thanks to Jane Cotton, Thalia Kidder, Maree Keating, and Sarah Totterdell)

Supplementary information (2)

Oxfam GB's rationale for work on gender equality
(Note: this is not a handout)

The rights-based approach

Human rights are tied inextricably to issues of gender equality. The Universal Declaration of Human Rights states unequivocally that men and women have equal human rights. Oxfam GB takes a rights-based approach to its work of addressing the root causes of poverty. Women and men, boys and girls, experience poverty when they are denied the rights to livelihoods, water, education, health care, protection and security, a voice in public life, or freedom from discrimination. Our definition of poverty goes beyond the purely economic to encompass capabilities, powerlessness, and inequity.

Addressing gender-based violations of human rights is a crucial aspect of Oxfam's development and anti-poverty work. Institutions and structures are predominantly shaped by and for men, and therefore they reflect existing inequalities and gendered power relations in society, and they also help to constitute them. By excluding women's voices, they work to the advantage of men as a group, and to the disadvantage of women. While recognising the many different ways in which women and men across the world are influenced by race, class, caste, colour, sexuality, age, religion, politics, disability, and other elements of identity, we can say that women's overall access to and power within institutions and structures is systemically limited because of gender inequality and discrimination.

> *However poverty is defined, there is one common feature: women are disproportionately affected... Whichever approach to poverty Oxfam takes, therefore, it must pay particular attention to gender inequity.*[1]

Poor women have less recourse than their male counterparts to legal and religious recognition and protection, as well as more limited access to public knowledge and information, and less power to make decisions about resources, both within and outside the home. Women in many parts of the world frequently have little control over their fertility, sexuality, and marital choices. This systemic discrimination reduces women's participation in public life, often increases their vulnerability to poverty, violence, and HIV infection, and results in their representing a disproportionate percentage of the poor population of the world.

Addressing human rights and gender inequality in our programmes

A focus on women's human rights can simultaneously address economic, social, civil, and political rights. In many instances, overcoming violence is the key to supporting women to achieve social and economic rights, such as the right to work and to achieve an adequate standard of living. Oxfam's programme work on violence against women has the potential to help women to achieve both social and economic rights (for example, access to HIV protection and health services, or to decent working conditions) as well as civil and political rights (for example, the freedom not to marry against their will, and the freedom not to be subject to cruel, inhuman, or degrading treatment).

---

[1] Definitions of poverty, Oxfam Fundamental Review Of Strategic Intent, Steering the course for the 21st century, 1998, 1.1.4

Many boys and men are also sometimes subject to gender-based violations of their human rights, particularly in situations where violent and risky behaviour is seen as evidence of masculinity. Working with men to examine what they gain and lose from their rigid gender-related roles can increase the impact of work on gender equality and women's rights. For example, in Brazil, Oxfam GB supports health and HIV programmes that have worked with groups of men to examine risky behaviour and address broader issues of gender equality.

Gender inequality and economic poverty

Women are not a homogeneous group. However, there is a universal factor weakening women's position vis-à-vis men in all major social institutions, namely, women's responsibility for reproductive work. By reproductive work is meant activities such as childcare, housework and cooking. Such work tends to be taken for granted and undervalued in all societies and economic systems. Both women's reproductive work burden itself, and the low value societies set on it, militate against gender equity.[2]

The effects of globalisation have had a devastating impact on the poor, and particularly on women. Unfair terms of trade under the rules of the World Trade Organisation have negatively affected agriculture and economies across the developing world, leading to falling incomes and widespread food insecurity. Adjustment policies, influenced by debt-reduction priorities and bilateral funding agreements, have resulted in cuts in public expenditure and reduced subsidies on basic services such as drinking water, food supply, health care, education, and transport. Women's multiple roles within the household and their role in subsistence food production, coupled with ideas, beliefs, and practices which discriminate against women, have culminated in a greater burden on women as workers and family care-givers. Cuts in social services, for example, have increased the burden on women as care-givers in the household. The introduction of user fees for health services in Zambia in the 1980s means that a sick person in a low-income household is more likely to be looked after by a female relative than taken to the clinic.

Most women do not have legal or traditional rights to land or other assets. They cannot get loans or credit, because they have no collateral. They cannot leave abusive men, because they are dependent on them for their economic survival and social status. In addition, they often lack the productive resources, including skills, information, and economic organisation, that they need in order to market their produce profitably. Women tend to be concentrated in the most risky, low-profit areas of marketing. If they lose their jobs or are unable to find employment due to global and local trends, women often seek inferior and less secure livelihoods in the informal sector, and/or though migration.

Economic policy and analysis tend to focus on productive work and the money economy, ignoring production for household consumption and the informal economy, where women predominate, as well as the unpaid work of caring for families and households. This leads to policies on aid, development, investment, and finance which both fail to promote development and further reinforce gender inequality through reaffirming cultural assumptions about women's roles. The view that productive work is men's responsibility, and consequently of greater value than women's work, is a serious barrier to development and detrimental to both sexes. Oxfam GB is committed to promoting a broader view of economics: one that values, protects, and promotes unpaid caring work as much as work in the cash economy.

---

[2] Geraldine Terry, Oxfam SCO 5 Strategic Framework Document, 2000

This has the dual impact of creating drastically improved development opportunities for men and women, and promoting gender equality.

In the transition economies of Eastern Europe, men have experienced absolute declines in life expectancies in recent years. This is associated with growing stress and anxiety, due to rapidly worsening unemployment among men.[3] The trafficking of women from the former Soviet Union to Europe is another impact of the same situation. A gender analysis will reveal the particular and different ways in which poverty affects women and men, and will enable the design of programmes to directly address the underlying causes of poverty, not merely the symptoms.

International trends influence the conditions of women's lives

With an **increase in religious fundamentalism** across the world, the rights of women have become a subject for extremist arguments. Women's right to organise, question, and debate in many countries is being curbed on the grounds of religious heresy and political disloyalty.

Widespread armed and ethnic conflict has gendered dimensions. Young boys, and often girls, in many conflict situations are compelled to leave school and risk their lives by engaging in dehumanising combat. Young girls are often forced into sexual slavery to service militia. Huge numbers of men are killed in combat, and women and children are killed and maimed as civilians. Women and girls form the majority of refugees or displaced populations, and the proportion of woman-maintained households in turbulent situations has increased. In addition, women in conflict situations suffer sexual assault and other forms of exploitation in the home during and after conflict. A large proportion of all Oxfam's programmes involves humanitarian and conflict work. In accordance with Humanitarian Charters, Oxfam recognises that humanitarian interventions are more effective when they are based on an understanding of men's and women's, boys' and girls' different needs, interests, vulnerabilities, capacities, and coping strategies, and the differing impacts of disaster upon them.

In many parts of the world **the AIDS epidemic** has become the single most important issue affecting development and poverty. There are strong links between the spread of HIV infection, gender equality, and gender-based violence. The fastest-growing group of those infected with AIDS is adolescent girls. In addition, the number of AIDS-related deaths has left a generation of orphans who are exposed to exploitation and high-risk behaviour. The extra burden of care is often placed on elderly women. These gender-related issues need to be considered together in all programme development.

---

[3] World Bank, Engendering Development Through Gender Equality in Rights, Resources, and Voice, 2001

Pick-up-and-Go Training Pack • Introduction to Gender Equality: Slides

Photo: Crispin Hughes

An Introduction to Gender Equality

Slide 1

PICK–UP–AND–GO

Module 1: Objectives

- **Know:** Understand how gender inequality relates to poverty, and why an NGO like Oxfam needs to promote it.

- **Feel:** Motivated to challenge gender discrimination, and mobilised to find out more about how to do this and to act.

- **Do:** Attempt a basic gender analysis of a case study.

PICK-UP-AND-GO

Suggested Ground Rules

Participants should:

1. Bring their own examples and points.

2. Listen to and respect others' views.

3. Respect others' right to confidentiality.

4. Be present throughout the course.

Slide 3

PICK-UP-AND-GO

45

Sex is...

- ...the biological difference between men and women.

- ... the same everywhere in the world.

Gender is...

- ...the attributes, roles, and activities connected to being a man or a woman.

- ...how women and men are perceived, and how they are expected to behave.

- ...different according to time, place, and culture.

Slide 4

PICK-UP-AND-GO

Mainstreaming gender equality is...

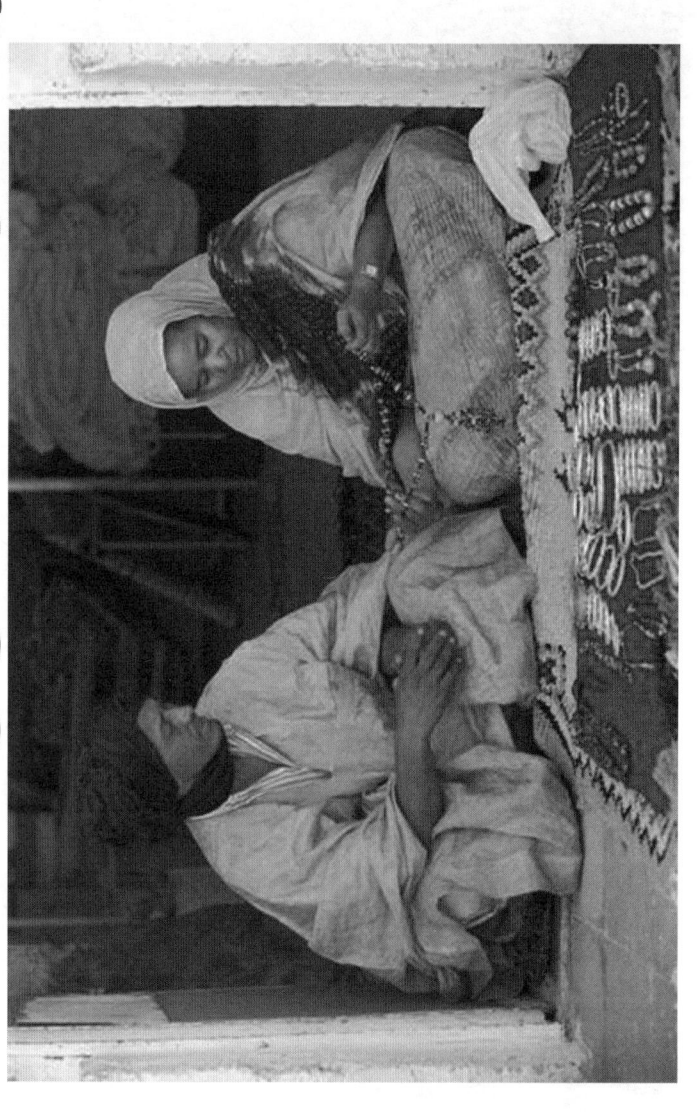

Photo: Ami Vitale

...the practical ways in which we all work towards gender equality

Slide 5

PICK–UP–AND–GO

Pick-up-and-Go Training Pack • Introduction to Gender Equality: Slides

For Oxfam,
gender-equality mainstreaming is ...

- A process of ensuring that all its work, and the way in which it is done, contributes to gender equality by transforming the balance of power between women and men.

Slide 6

Women's needs can be ...

Practical:

- Immediate perceived needs, e.g. for better living conditions, improved health services, water, food, and education.

Or Strategic:

- Gender imbalances in power relations, such as those related to labour, legal rights, domestic violence, access and control, e.g. the fact that women have to look after children affects their capacity to earn an income.

Slide 7

PICK-UP-AND-GO

Pick-up-and-Go Training Pack • Introduction to Gender Equality: Slides

Is this fair?

Gender Equality Quiz

PICK-UP-AND-GO

51

1. Rank these five countries by the representation of women in their National Assembly/ Parliament. Highest proportion first.

- Rwanda
- Sweden
- UK
- Tanzania
- Uganda

Slide 10

2. The five countries ranked according to the representation of women in their National Assembly/ Parliament. Highest proportion first.

Country	% of women	world rank
• Rwanda	48.8	1
• Sweden	45	2
• Uganda	24.7	18
• Tanzania	22.3	20
• UK	17.9	33

Slide 11

PICK-UP-AND-GO

53

3. How much of the world's property is owned by women and girls?

- Just over 10%
- Just under 5%
- Just under 1%

Slide 12

4. Percentage of the world's property owned by women and girls:

- Just under 1%

Slide 13

5. Across the world, of all children currently out of school, what proportion are girls?

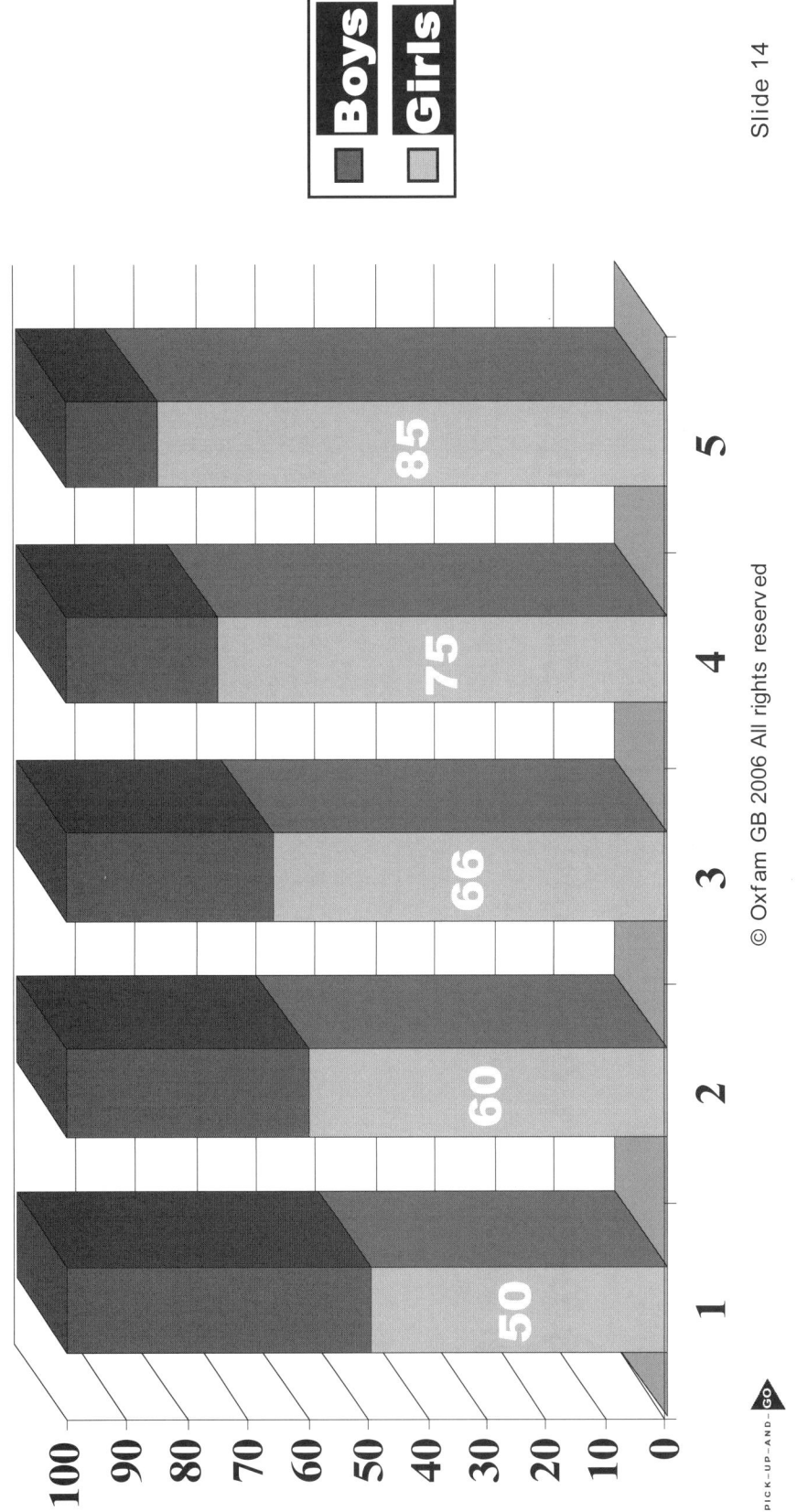

Boys
Girls

Slide 14

PICK–UP–AND–GO

6. The proportion of children currently out of school who are girls.

Currently more than 100 million children of primary-school age are not in school.

85% of those children are girls.

Slide 15

PICK–UP–AND–GO

7. Across the world, what percentage of women will be raped at least once?

- 2 – 5 %
- 10 – 15%
- 15 – 20%
- 20 – 25%

Slide 16

8. Across the world, what percentage of women will be raped at least once?

15 – 20%

PICK-UP-AND-GO

The women of our world...

Photo: Shailan Parker

- Work 70% of all hours worked.

- Produce half of all our food.

- Earn 10% of our income.

- Make up 75% of illiterates.

- Are only 14% of members of parliament.

- Are 8% of cabinet ministers.

Is this just?...

Slide 18

PICK-UP-AND-GO

Where are the missing girls?

- 100 million girls are estimated as missing due to preferences for sons, and the killing of girls before or after birth through sex-selective abortion, infanticide, selective malnourishment, and lack of health care.

(Source: The Atlas of Women, Joni Seager, The Women's Press, 2003.)

Slide 19

PICK–UP–AND–GO

Oxfam's Gender Policy is a commitment to …..

- base its work on the understanding that gender equality is key to overcoming poverty and suffering.

- work with women and men to address specific ideas and beliefs that create and reinforce gender-related poverty.

- empower women in all aspects of the programme and ways of working, and prioritise work that raises the status of women.

- ensure that internal practices and ways of working reflect a commitment to gender equality.

Slide 20

PICK–UP–AND–GO

PICK-UP-AND-GO

Mainstreaming Gender Equality
in NGOs

8 hours

Written by Elsa Dawson
(formerly Oxfam GB Gender Adviser for South America)
with help, support, and contributions from many Oxfam staff around the world

Mainstreaming Gender Equality in NGOs

Contents

Facilitator's notes

Handouts

Supplementary information

PowerPoint slides 96

Facilitator's notes

Introduction

Information for managers
Length of workshop 8 hours, including lunch and breaks: one day
Facilitation skills This workshop requires presentation skills and the management of both facilitated discussion and small-group activities. The facilitator must have experience of mainstreaming gender equality in development, humanitarian, or advocacy programmes. Alternatively, a good facilitator could run the course with a support person present who has gender-mainstreaming experience. Managers are responsible for ensuring that this workshop is delivered by a member of staff of sufficient capability.
Learners This workshop is intended for all staff who need to understand how they can improve the mainstreaming of gender equality in their programme and their organisation's culture and systems.
Preparation by learners It is assumed that participants have some understanding of gender equality. For those staff who do not, this pack includes a separate Pick-up-and-Go module for a half-day course: *Introduction to Gender Equality*.
Size of group This workshop could be run for groups of 3–20, but it is easier for learners to ask questions and easier for facilitators to manage the activities if groups are smaller: ideally 6–12 members.

Information for facilitators
Room This workshop requires space for the whole group to work together in a room – sitting in such a way that they can all see one another. It also requires sufficient space for the group to break into smaller groups of about five persons.
Equipment needed ■ Flipchart stand and paper. ■ Laptop and data projector; or an overhead projector with PowerPoint slides printed on to acetates. ■ Flipchart pens. ■ Cards (big enough to write something which will be legible if stuck up on the wall). ■ Some means of attaching paper and cards to the wall, e.g. Blutack, pins, or sticky tape.

Preparation of material

1. Photocopy the agenda and handouts.
   - Handout 1: Dominican Republic coffee-production case study (for Session 3)
   - Handout 2: Humanitarian-relief scenario (for Session 4)
   - Handout 3: Evaluation form (for Session 6)

2. Copy the PowerPoint slides on to acetate transparencies
   (unless you are using a data projector).

3. Write the agenda for the day on a flipchart sheet and display it on the wall where
   all participants can see it. Use this to guide them through the day.

Supplementary Information

These documents provide you with checklists and potential answers for some of the
exercises, to help you to support the learners. **They are not intended for use as
lecturing material or as handouts for participants.** (You are a facilitator, not a
lecturer.)

For this workshop, you should have the following briefs:

1. 'Gender in the programme-management cycle' (for Session 2)
2. 'Capacities and vulnerabilities: possible answers to the humanitarian-relief
   scenario exercise' (for Session 4)
3. 'How gender equality can be mainstreamed in key elements of our
   organisational culture and systems' (for Session 5)

Linked learning

Books:
- *The Oxfam Gender Training Manual*, Suzanne Williams with Janet Seed and
  Adelina Mwau, Oxford: Oxfam GB, 1995.
- *A Guide to Gender-Analysis Frameworks*, Candida March, Ines Smyth, and
  Maitrayee Mukhopadhyay, Oxford: Oxfam GB, 1999.
- *Gender Works: Oxfam Experience in Policy and Practice*, Fenella Porter, Ines
  Smyth, and Caroline Sweetman (eds.), Oxford: Oxfam GB, 1999.
- *Gender Equality and Men: Learning from Practice*, Sandy Ruxton (ed.), Oxford:
  Oxfam GB, 2004.

Internet:
- www.undp.org/gender/ Contains UNDP gender-mainstreaming information and
  tools.
- www.unifem.org News and resources on gender and development issues.
- www.worldbank.org/gender/ The GenderNet, providing information and
  experience on gender and development.

People:
For Oxfam staff, expert support on gender is available from Regional Gender
Advisers, the Programme Policy Team, and the Humanitarian Department Gender
Adviser.

> **Translations**
>
> This workshop is currently available in English, Spanish, French, and Portuguese. If it would help learners, please feel free to translate all or part of this into additional languages – but please send a copy to the Oxfam Publishing team at Oxfam House in the UK.
>
> **Support and feedback**
>
> Please send questions, ideas, and feedback to learninternational@oxfam.org.uk

Workshop objectives

As a result of taking part in the workshop, participants will:

Know …

The key elements of work to mainstream gender equality in programmes and organisational culture.

Feel …

Motivated to ensure that all aspects of their work contribute to gender equality by transforming the balance of power between women and men, and committed to challenge gender discrimination wherever it is found.

Do …

Use a case study to practise steps in mainstreaming gender equality into a project. As a result of this workshop, participants will understand that NGOs like Oxfam are concerned to address the injustice faced by poor women throughout the world, and to challenge the abuse of their rights. They will understand why we cannot effectively and sustainably alleviate poverty without addressing related gender inequality.

This is a basic workshop for use with all kinds of staff, but it can be adapted to respond to the precise requirements of particular participants.

Optional pre-course questionnaire

It may help you if you know in advance the participants' expectations and current levels of knowledge. You could find out by asking the questions below, either face-to-face or by telephone. Asking such questions will also help you to establish a trusting relationship with individual participants on a sometimes sensitive subject.

1. Have you attended any other Gender Training course?
2. What do you hope to learn from this workshop?
3. What are the main gender-related issues that you encounter in your work?

Case study

Case studies are provided as a basis for this course. They have been carefully designed to be relevant in most geographical contexts. If you feel that it would make your workshops more effective, you could replace them with more relevant texts, but you should use the following criteria when choosing them.

1. They should include clear examples of the relationship between poverty and gender inequality.
2. They should be no longer than one page in length, or six PowerPoint slides.
3. The case study for Session 3 should illustrate a number of replicable ways of mainstreaming gender equality effectively.
4. The case study for Session 4 should provide information on the differing capacities and vulnerabilities of women and men in a given group of potential beneficiaries.

Timetable

Start	Finish	Session
0000	0045	1. Introductions
0045	0215	2. Mainstreaming gender equality in the project and programme management cycle
0215	0230	BREAK
0230	0345	3. Mainstreaming gender equality: a case study of good practice
0345	0445	LUNCH
0445	0645	4. Gender analysis
0645	0700	BREAK
0700	0745	5. Mainstreaming gender equality in organisational culture and systems
0745	0800	6. Course evaluation

The timings for this eight-hour event are shown as starting from 00.00. The actual start-time will depend on the group's normal working hours.

Note to facilitator

The subject of gender can stimulate many questions and debates. Many useful lessons can come out of such discussions, but it is important to move the course along and delay questions until the relevant part of the course – when they may be covered anyway.

- Pay careful attention to the timings of the workshop, and chair the sessions strictly. Explain to the participants that not every question can be asked or answered in the time allowed.

- Put up a page of flipchart paper on the wall and use it to 'park' questions that cannot be answered immediately. This is a way of acknowledging the question. Explain how answers will be provided: for example, by referring it to an appropriate colleague.

- In order to maintain the pace of the course, it is important to provide clear instructions and information about timings. Five minutes before the end of each group exercise, tell the learners that five minutes remain; one minute before the end, tell them that they have one more minute. Always finish the session on time. Groups working under pressure tend to produce better results.

- During group work, circulate among the groups to make sure that they have understood the exercise and are working effectively.

Session 1

Introductions

TOTAL TIME: 45 minutes

Purpose: to introduce everyone to each other and to the goals of the workshop.

Timing	What YOU do	What the LEARNERS do	Resources
00.00	• Welcome everyone, introduce yourself, show Slide 1. • Ask the participants to introduce themselves briefly, stating their name, their role, and the reason why they are attending this workshop.	• Introduce themselves by giving their name, their role, and their reason for being here.	**Slide 1**

00.15	• Show the following, asking for comments and suggestions on each:
	   ○ Slide 2: Objectives for this workshop
	   ○ Agenda (written on a flipchart sheet and displayed on the wall)
	   ○ Slide 3: Suggested ground rules.
	
	• Show Slide 4 ('Which project is gender-mainstreamed?') and discuss the answer with participants. 'Leadership training programme', with a crèche facility', 'Providing a refuge for women escaping violence', and 'Supporting single fathers with child care' could all be examples of gender mainstreaming, depending on the particular analysis of gender. 'Providing income-generation opportunities for a village community' is not apparently concerned with the specific needs of either sex.
		• Check that they agree with each of these, and express any concerns and suggestions.
		
		• Explain what mainstreaming gender equality means in their own work.
			Slide 2: 'Workshop objectives'
			
			Slide 3: 'Suggested ground rules'
			
			Slide 4: 'Which project is gender-mainstreamed?'
			
			Slide 5: 'Oxfam's definition of gender mainstreaming'

00.45	• Show Slide 5 (the Oxfam GB definition) and ask participants to describe examples from their own work and ways of working – but keep this discussion short.		

Session 2   Mainstreaming gender equality in the project and programme management cycle (2 pages)

Total time: 1 hour 30 minutes

Purpose: to provide participants with clear ideas for integrating gender equality into their programme-management work.

Timing	What YOU do	What the LEARNERS do	Resources
00.45	• Show Slide 6 and explain that Oxfam GB is mainstreaming gender equality into its programmes and into the organisation. Both aspects will be considered in today's workshop. • Show Slide 7 and explain that gender equality is included in Oxfam's Strategic Change Objectives in two ways: both as a separate objective ('SCO 5') and mainstreamed into all of the others. • Show Slide 8 to present the text of SCO 5. • For Oxfam staff: ask participants to explain briefly how the overall framework presented on the slide is being interpreted in the programme where they work. How is gender equality being integrated in each SCO that their Region is working on? Do regional Programme Implementation Plans (PIPs) adequately reflect the integration of gender equality?	• Check that they understand the way in which gender equality is treated in Oxfam GB's Strategic Change Objectives. • Explain how their Region is interpreting this framework.	**Slides 6 and 7** on the integration of gender equality in Oxfam GB **Slide 8:** 'SCO 5'
01.00	• Show the simplified example of a programme and project management cycle on Slide 9 to stimulate discussion. • Divide the participants into groups. Allocate one of the stages to each. If there are insufficient participants, allocate two stages to each group. Ensure that each group includes at least one programme staff member. • Ask them to produce a list of gender-related tasks that they are doing, or tasks that could usefully be done, at each stage in the cycle, in order to integrate gender equality more effectively into	• Brainstorm ideas on what is being done and what could usefully be done at each stage of the programme/project management cycle in order to integrate gender equality into all activities.	**Slide 9:** 'Simplified programme/project management cycle'

Timing	What YOU do	What the LEARNERS do	Resources
	the programme. Ask them to consider development, humanitarian, and advocacy work, and ask Oxfam staff to describe how they are applying gender-related considerations to their use of the Oxfam Programme Accountability and Learning (OPAL) system.		
	• Use the checklist in Supplementary Information (1): 'Gender equality in the programme management cycle' to stimulate group discussions.		
	• Ask each group to agree the three most important tasks.	• Agree the most important tasks with other members of their groups.	
	• Hold a plenary feedback session in which each group presents its members' view of the most important tasks to be carried out at the stages that they discussed.	• Present these to a plenary session.	
02.15	• Show Slide 10 and emphasise that if gender equality is incorporated in the analysis stage of programme management, it will logically fall into the rest of the programme and its development. This is why a whole session will be dedicated to gender analysis. Emphasise that this applies also to advocacy and humanitarian work.		**Slide 10:** 'Incorporating gender equality into Programme Implementation Plans'

02.15-02.30	BREAK
Remember that a break is an important aspect of learning. Encourage the group to get up and walk around, but ask them not to get involved in other work such as making telephone calls.	

Session 3 Mainstreaming gender equality: a case study of good practice
(2 pages)

Total time: 1 hour 15 minutes

Purpose: to engage participants in a practical exercise to practise integrating gender equality into programme and project management.

Timing	What YOU do	What the LEARNERS do	Resources

02.30	• Give out copies of Handout 1.
	• Ask learners to return to their groups and discuss the way in which gender equality has been mainstreamed in this project. What was done well, and what could be improved on? How could the tasks that they identified in the previous session improve the integration of gender equality in this project? How did this project involve men in the work of redressing gender imbalances?
	• Here are some criticisms which they might make:
	  ○ The FEDECARES programme failed to include gender equality from the start, and did not carry out a gender analysis at the beginning.
	  ○ Therefore the staff did not consider the specific needs of men and women from the start.
	  ○ Doing this might have led the programme to focus on ways of addressing inequalities in terms of the women's unequal work burdens, and the unequal returns that women received for their work.
	  ○ We are not told whether the women were paid for their labour; if not, what was being done about it? We are not told how their work could have been made easier.
	  ○ Nothing was done to give women the time that they needed to participate in decision-making.
		• Practise applying and defending the application of tasks that they defined in the previous session, by judging the strengths and weaknesses in a real-life case of gender-equality mainstreaming.	**Handout 1:** 'Dominican Republic case study'

Timing	What YOU do	What the LEARNERS do	Resources
	• Ask them to prepare to report their conclusions in the form of a dialogue between one member of each group in his or her Oxfam role, speaking to another member of the group, who plays the role of the Director of FEDECARES.		
	• Explain that the Director of FEDECARES is anxious to defend the project and the way that it has mainstreamed gender equality. The Director questions the usefulness of implementing Oxfam's suggestions.	• Divide into small groups and take 30 minutes to prepare a 10-minute role-play.	
	• Give them 30 minutes for their group work, telling them to prepare a ten-minute role-play.		
	• If there is resistance to the idea of a role-play, ask each group to report back its conclusions on a flipchart.		
3.00	• Conduct a plenary session in which each small group presents its ten-minute role-play.	• Share their ideas in the form of a role-play presented to the other groups.	
3.40	• Once all the feedback is complete, ask participants what they have learned from this exercise in terms of relating effectively to partners on the subject of mainstreaming gender equality in projects that they support or implement.		
3.45			

3.45-4.45	LUNCH
	Remember that a break is an important aspect of learning. Encourage participants to get up and to walk around, but ask them not to get involved in other work such as making telephone calls.

Session 4   Gender analysis

(3 pages)

Total time: 2 hours

Purpose: to introduce the basic elements of gender analysis, and give an opportunity to try out a key gender-analysis framework.

Timing	What YOU do	What the LEARNERS do	Resources
04.45	• Ask participants what they understand by 'gender analysis'. Check their answers against Slide 11 (the Oxfam definition). • Show Slide 12. • Ask the participants to form pairs in which both members have knowledge of a particular group of beneficiaries. • Invite them to consider the basic gender-analysis questions on Slide 12 and apply them to this particular group. Give them 15 minutes. • Ask one person from each pair to mention one new fact about gender inequality that they have learned from this discussion.	• Explore what they understand by gender analysis, and apply the basic questions to a group of beneficiaries with whom they are familiar.	**Slide 11:** 'Definition of gender analysis' **Slide 12:** 'Gender analysis – basic questions'
05.15	• Show Slide 13. The Capacities and Vulnerabilities framework, disaggregated by sex, is especially useful in humanitarian work, but it can be applied to other situations, to help to plan the relief of immediate needs, and to help people to develop strengths for their future development. (The original source of the framework is *Rising from the Ashes; Development Strategies in Times of Disaster*, by Mary B Anderson and Peter J Woodrow, published by UNESCO and Westview Press, 1989.) • The exercise will help participants to think about the differences (both positive and negative) between the situations of women and men, and how women's needs and strengths are ignored in interventions that are not gender-sensitive. • Explain how to use the framework, using the following definitions. **Capacities:** existing strengths of individuals and social groups. **Vulnerabilities:** long-term factors which weaken people's ability to cope. These factors exist before and after disasters. They are different from immediate needs in that they require the long-term strategic solutions that are part of development work.		**Slide 13:** 'Capacities and Vulnerabilities framework'

Timing	What YOU do	What the LEARNERS do	Resources
	Physical or material capacities and vulnerabilities: features of the land, climate, and environment where people live, their health, skills, work, housing, technologies, water and food supplies, access to capital and other assets. Ask participants to think about who has access to and control over these resources. **Social or organisational capacities and vulnerabilities:** the social fabric of a community, formal political structures, informal decision-making and leadership systems, and systems for organising any social and economic activities, at both the family and community levels. **Motivational and attitudinal capacities and vulnerabilities:** cultural and psychological factors, which might be related to religion, or a community's history of crisis, and their expectation of emergency or developmental assistance.		
5.30	**Group work** • Ask participants to form groups of four or five people. Ideally, they should apply the framework to a group of beneficiaries with whom they are working or familiar, because the exercise demands detailed knowledge of their situation. However, if no such group can be cited, the Humanitarian-Relief Scenario (Handout 2) can be used, and learners should use their imagination to decide what the different capacities and vulnerabilities of the female and male refugees might be. • Give them 45 minutes to create a capacities and vulnerabilities analysis. • Alternatively, if more time is available, use the case study of El Salvador refugees on page 395 of the *Oxfam Gender Training Manual*. It provides more details and leaves less to the imagination; but it is quite long, so do not use it if members of the group tend to read slowly. • Ask each group to elect a spokesperson. Give them flipchart paper on which to complete the boxes of the matrix, to present the results of their discussions to a plenary. • During the group work, go round the groups to check that each has correctly understood the categories of the framework and the object of the exercise.	• Work in small groups, using a key gender-analysis framework	**Handout 2:** 'Humanitarian scenario' Flipchart sheets

Timing	What YOU do	What the LEARNERS do	Resources

6.15	**Plenary session**
	• Ask one group to report their results for one part of the framework. Then ask if the other groups had any different answers.
	• Then invite another group to share their results for the next part of the framework, and so on.
	• In your summing up, you could make the following points:
	    ○ This exercise helps us to identify the differences between the situations of men and women.
	    ○ We need detailed information about the exact nature and situation of beneficiaries, in order to plan effective interventions.
	    ○ Gender relations might change in conflict and emergency situations. Applying the matrix at different points in time, for example to a group of people before they flee their homes and afterwards, can be useful for showing this.
	    ○ Ignoring women's capacities may lead to negative discrimination and inefficiency.
		Groups take turns to share their analysis	

06.45			

6.45 – 7.00	BREAK
	Remember that a break is an important aspect of learning . Encourage the group to get up and walk around, but ask them not to get involved in other work such as making telephone calls

Session 5 Mainstreaming gender equality in an organisation's culture and systems

Total time: 45 minutes

Purpose: to develop participants' ideas about how to make their organisational culture more conducive to the mainstreaming of gender equality in the programme.

Timing	What YOU do	What the LEARNERS do	Resources
7.00	• Show Slide 14 and explain that, having thought about ways in which gender equality is mainstreamed in programme work, they are now going to consider how gender equality can be mainstreamed in an organisation's culture and systems. • Ask them to consider what their organisation's culture and systems do to make it either easy or hard to integrate gender equality into the programme. • Show Slide 15 and ask them to consider this question in relation to each section.	• Consider which aspects of organisational culture could be improved in order to integrate gender equality more effectively into the programme – and how.	**Slides 14, 15:** Mainstreaming gender equality in Oxfam GB and in its organisational culture
7.15 7.45	• Ask the participants to form a group for each of the four parts of the triangle shown on Slide 15, and brainstorm ideas for how to improve the mainstreaming of gender equality in each. • A checklist of ideas for each element is provided in Supplementary Information (3), which you can use to stimulate these discussions.		

Session 6

Total time:
15 minutes

Course evaluation

Purpose: to review the workshop and plan how the participants will use their learning in the workplace.

Timing	What YOU do	What the LEARNERS do	Resources
07.45	• Ask each participant to draft a performance objective to show how they will mainstream gender equality in their work, in the light of what they have learned in this workshop. Tell them that they have 5 minutes to write their objectives. • Ask each participant to share his or her objective with the rest of the group.	• Decide on the main new thing that they will do as a result of taking this workshop, and comment on any changes that they will need to make in the way that they work.	
08.00	• Ask the participants to complete the evaluation form (Handout 3) before they leave the room.	• Complete the evaluation form.	**Handout 3:** 'Evaluation form'

Handout 1:
Dominican Republic coffee-production case study
(two pages)

Fedecares is a federation of more than 6,000 small-scale coffee producers in 120 rural communities in the poor mountainous south of the Dominican Republic. It was created in 1985 and began working with Oxfam GB the following year.

Miladis Mateo,
Fedecares supervisor:

'Life continues to be difficult for women. A lot has to change, but it's not only up to us.'

Photo: Pedro Guzman/Oxfam

Up to 1995, Oxfam supported institutional development, leadership, and technical training for coffee production and marketing. From 1995, it began to pay greater attention to gender relations in the organisation, encouraging meetings for women coffee producers, and women's participation in leadership workshops.

Oxfam researched the different roles that men and women play in coffee production, and the factors limiting women's participation in the federation. Women coffee producers describe their day-to-day lives and their disadvantages as follows:

'Women are essential to small-scale coffee production. We work side by side with our husbands and children. We give logistical support at harvest time. We get breakfast ready at daybreak. Then we start preparing lunch. We help to collect the coffee beans. At mid-day we go back to the kitchen to finish lunch. Later in the afternoon we spend hours peeling and washing the coffee beans and putting them out to dry on the terrace. Some women go with their husbands to sell the coffee. But usually selling is men's business.'

'It's difficult for women to take part in meetings, because we have to do all the housework and look after the children. Many of us are illiterate, and we get bored in the meetings. But there are some who know how to write and to be leaders just as well as the men.'

On the basis of the research, Oxfam initiated a series of steps to improve women's participation in training and development opportunities.

1. **Dialogue and training.** Oxfam began discussions with the leaders of Fedecares about the importance of mainstreaming gender equality in the federation. The leaders were persuaded to participate in workshops on gender and development.
2. **Accompaniment in decision-making processes**. Fedecares showed a general understanding of concepts of gender equality, but found it difficult to design and implement processes for gender mainstreaming. Oxfam staff accompanied them through a period of gender-sensitisation which taught them to take decisions that effectively contribute to gender equality.

3. **Applying positive discrimination in projects**. A gender analysis identified the need for work specifically designed to improve women's situation.
4. Finally, **indicators on gender equality** were developed to enable progress monitoring and the identification of barriers to gender mainstreaming.

At the beginning, it was necessary to promote the principles of gender-equality mainstreaming quite forcefully. Resistance to change was encountered, so it was important not to push the process too quickly, but to educate people at every stage.

In 1995, the level of women's participation was very low. Women were not members of the federation, nor were they included in management teams. Their involvement in decision making was extremely limited. At the Fedecares offices, women were employed only as accounting assistants, secretaries, and receptionists, and no woman had management responsibilities. Fedecares changed its statutes to promote the participation of women. Membership was no longer given to an individual (usually a male landowner) as it had been previously, but to the family unit. Any family member could now represent the family at meetings of the association or federation. Women's participation in educational activities and meetings increased substantially: at the most recent general assembly, 25 per cent of delegates were women. Since 1996 all management committees have included women, and in 1998 the number of women in the decision-making structures of Fedecares was increased as part of the institutional capacity-building process. Of the three current managers, one is a woman.

Fedecares staff also participated in gender training on gender identity; self-esteem, prejudices, and gender stereotypes; sex and gender; equal opportunities; human rights and women's human rights; and gender and development.

Roque Feliz, Programme Co-ordinator, Dominican Republic

Handout 2: Humanitarian-relief scenario

(This scenario is fictional, but is loosely based on the real facts of real situations.)

Severe abuses of human rights in Ruritania had caused an estimated 20,000 people to flee across the mountainous border into neighbouring Moritania, where they faced new hardships. They fled increased militarisation, the destruction of their villages, forced labour, confiscation of their land, and generally degrading and inhumane treatment, including sexual violence against women and girls. The government of Ruritania had imposed martial law and imprisoned anyone who criticised it, leading to the persecution of many opposition activists and village leaders. Many had male relatives who had been savagely killed in attacks on their villages, or who joined up with the opposition forces, leaving widows and orphans behind to cope on their own.

The refugees were mainly small traders and livestock farmers. For food, they grew maize, beans, and a limited range of vegetables. Women would look after poultry and goats, while men herded cows. Boys had a two-in-three chance of attending primary school, and half as many girls attended as boys. Only 15 per cent of adults could read or write. Some of the men had worked as tailors.

The government of Moritania invited international aid agencies to come in and assist the refugees. The UNHCR and a number of international NGOs set up refugee camps just south of the border. These were intended to house refugees for a few days before they were moved on; but because there was nowhere else for them to go, they were staying in the camps for months on end.

The refugees arriving at the camps were traumatised and exhausted, having suffered more brutality in the no-man's land between the borders at the hands of the Moritanian police, who packed them into buses to send them to the camps without any explanation about where they were going. Stripped of their identity documents, they faced a very difficult future, whether they stayed or whether they returned to Ruritania and tried to reclaim their land, property, and citizenship. High proportions were women and children and female-headed households, and there were many who were disabled and sick.

Conditions in the muddy, smelly camps were appalling. All relief agencies were strained beyond their capacity to care for the sudden influx of refugees. Tents were erected in straight lines and close together, the largest ones accommodating 70 people with no privacy or protection. There was no artificial lighting, and the site was not planned in accordance with the demographic composition of the refugees. Sanitation facilities were wholly inadequate, and provided little privacy. No safe spaces had been set up for children, who stumbled about in the mud among the 4-wheel drives, large trucks, and earth-moving equipment. People were living on dry rations and any fresh food that the agencies could bring in. There was no space provided for the refugees to cook for themselves, and they would spend hours each day in queues waiting for a meal.

Handout 3: Course evaluation

(for Session 6)

Name (optional): _____ **Date:** _____

For each question where there is a scale, please circle the relevant number.

1. **I understand what mainstreaming gender equality means for an organisation like Oxfam GB.**

2. **I understand how I can integrate gender equality into my work.**

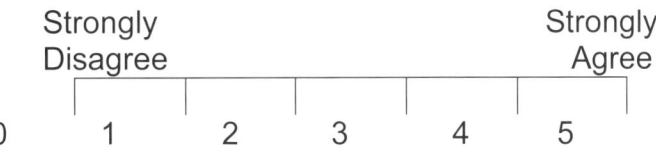

3. **I understand the basic principles of gender analysis and how they can be applied.**

Is there anything that could be done differently to raise any of the scores you have given?
How could the facilitator improve their skills in helping others to learn?

Supplementary information

These notes provide background information, checklists, and potential answers for some of the exercises, to help you to support participants on the course. They are not intended for use as lecturing material or to hand out to participants.

For this module, you need the following supplementary documents:

1. Gender equality in the programme-management cycle (for Session 2)
2. Capacities and vulnerabilities – possible answers to the humanitarian-relief scenario exercise (for Session 4)
3. How gender equality can be mainstreamed in key elements of organisational culture and systems (for Session 5)

Supplementary information (1) (for Session 2)

Gender equality in the programme-management cycle

(This is not a handout)

This checklist is based on Oxfam GB's booklet of Gender Mainstreaming Tools, produced by Fiona Gell and Paresh Motla.

Needs assessment (for humanitarian work)

- Collect sex-disaggregated data, remembering that emergencies may affect men and women in different ways.
- Look out for ways in which women and girls have become more vulnerable, ways in which their inequality has worsened, and what their specific needs are, both practical and strategic.
- Identify ways in which they have developed new capacities (different from those of men) as a result of the emergency. Emergencies may be opportunities for developing such capacities and redressing gender-related imbalances of power.

Situation analysis

What:
Conduct a gender-sensitive poverty analysis in relation to the programme or project theme, using sex-disaggregated data that illustrate the following:

- How the situation of poor women differs from that of poor men. Any differences in terms of their skills, capacities, and aspirations.
- Ways in which gender inequality relates to poverty.
- Who takes the decisions and who has power?
- Who has access to and control over resources?
- What practical and strategic needs do women and men have?
- The ability of women to exercise their human rights (with reference to agreements such as the Universal Declaration of Human Rights, the Beijing Platform for Action, and the Convention on the Elimination of all Forms of Discrimination against Women).
- Numbers of women-headed households, and their particular situations.

Analyse the ways in which policies, practices, ideas, and beliefs affect women and men in different ways.

How:
- Actively involve women, men, girls, and boys from diverse social groups in the analysis.
- Identify reliable existing sources of information on women's specific situation, such as local gender specialists, UNIFEM, NGOs that focus on women's issues, and existing gender studies.
- Ensure that terms of reference for any additional research that is commissioned include the need for a gender-sensitive analysis, and ensure that researchers have adequate skills to do this.

Planning, designing, redesigning

What:
- Ensure that all objectives and strategies proposed will address and reduce the poverty-related gender inequality identified in the analysis.
- Identify and categorise intended beneficiaries according to their sex.
- Ensure that activity plans show how equal participation by male and female beneficiaries will be organised.
- Check that budgets reflect gender-specific activities: for example, women-targeted projects, or initiatives to engage men in gender-equality work.
- Assess the potential impact of the project or programme on women and men, both positive and negative: for example, will it increase women's workload? Will it give men preferential access to project resources or decision-making forums?
- Include monitoring indicators that measure changes in gender equality, and collect relevant baseline data.

How:
- Plan with the active participation of women, both beneficiaries and members of partner organisations, incorporating their proposals and the development of their capacity.
- Ensure that beneficiaries and partner organisations are aware of your organisation's objective of challenging gender inequality.

Appraisal of partner organisation(s)
- Examine the capacity and potential of the partner organisation to mainstream gender equality throughout its programmes and institutional practices.
- Consider whether the project or programme will contribute to your organisation's goals on gender equality.
- Select partners with the best capacity for gender-sensitive programme management, or the strongest interest in developing this capacity.

Novib Oxfam Netherlands has developed a set of criteria, known as 'Traffic Lights', for judging how well partner organisations are mainstreaming gender equality into their work. The criteria are divided into three phases, which are likely to represent the progressive development of gender sensitivity of an organisation.

Novib's 'traffic lights' criteria for assessing the mainstreaming of gender equality in partner organisations

Phase 1
- Gender-disaggregated baseline monitoring, evaluation, and impact information is collected, analysed, and used to inform programme development.

- Female and male beneficiaries participate equally in decision making when projects are planned, implemented, and evaluated, and their opinions are reflected in the way that programme decisions are made.

- Staff and volunteers have a sufficient level of understanding and skill to enable a basic gender analysis to be carried out.

Phase 2
- A rights-based gender analysis that demonstrates the links between poverty, discrimination against women, and gender inequality is developed, and this analysis is reflected in the organisation's policy and programme.
- There is a balance of women and men in senior and middle management; or the organisation is actively seeking to redress an imbalance in order to reflect its beneficiary population more equitably. Women and men understand the need for gender-balanced decision making and are able to ensure that decisions taken reflect their different interests.

Phase 3
- A significant number of male staff members and beneficiaries are actively engaged in work to strengthen gender equality.
- The organisation actively exchanges knowledge and information, collaborates with others to extend and share its learning on gender issues, and uses this learning to shape its programme.
- The organisation challenges gender-stereotyped beliefs and discriminatory attitudes towards women, both in its internal practices and externally.

Implementation
Ensure that …
- Female beneficiaries and partner organisation staff are as actively involved in the management of the project as male counterparts.
- Female and male beneficiaries and staff of partner organisations have equal access to information, resources, and opportunities to carry out their responsibilities in the programme or project.
- Women's participation does not merely serve to increase their workload, but consists of active involvement in decision making concerning the management of the project.
- Work on gender equality is also carried out with men.

Strengthen the capacity of programme or project implementers in gender-sensitive programme management.

Monitoring, evaluation, and impact assessment
Ensure that there is a monitoring and evaluation system in place which will enable staff to identify positive and negative impact in terms of gender equality, including the following:

- The equal participation of women and men in decision-making processes in private and public spheres.
- Equal access for women and men to resources, equal control over resources, and equal access to basic social services.
- The incidence of gender-related violence against women.
- Women's empowerment (confidence, self-esteem, capacity for leadership and self-organisation).
- Gender stereotypes and discriminatory attitudes towards women and girls. This includes changes in the understanding and commitment of men to supporting women's empowerment (as measured by women and men separately).

If gender-impact indicators were developed at the planning stage, use these to assess progress. If not, develop them now.

Supplementary information (2) (for Session 4)

Capacities and Vulnerabilities: possible answers to humanitarian-relief scenario exercise

	Capacities		Vulnerabilities	
	Women	**Men**	**Women**	**Men**
Physical/ Material	Skills in caring for sick children and other adults under difficult circumstances. Skills in baking, herbal remedy preparation, trading small items, care of small livestock. Some women-headed households able to take on traditionally male roles, others unable to. Some women trained as primary-school teachers and traditional midwives.	Skills in trading and cow herding. Some able to generate income by selling food rations or blankets, or labouring on nearby farms. Some have skills in tailoring.	Inadequate security, for example when using sanitation facilities; unequal access to water, sanitation, shelter, food. Difficulties in caring for sick family members and children, and coping with high level of disease. Female-headed households suffering particular hardship, e.g. having to care for orphans.	Inadequate access to water, sanitation, shelter, food. Few income generation opportunities.
Social/ Organisational	Community leadership and organisational capacities, e.g. in forming small groups to work land collectively.	Social and political leadership skills. Run refugee committees. Communal traditions concerning exchange of food and shelter.	27 per cent of households led by a woman. Camp resources distributed to men. Need to provide sexual favours in exchange for resources.	Most men too exhausted and their morale too low to exercise their skills effectively.
Motivational/ Attitudinal	Religious faith strengthened women's survival capacity under harsh conditions. Their lives had not been easy back in Ruritania, where the conflict had raged for many years, so they were used to coping with crises.	Some men able to find work. Main type of support requested was in income generation. Some men had established schools where women teachers were providing children with educational activities.	Women and girls traumatised by experience of violence, including sexual violence. Those who lost husbands and children in the attacks were particularly affected. Some had developed signs of mental illness.	Morale low following the violence witnessed. Depressed by lack of employment opportunities and fears for the future. Fear of reprisals also affected their state of mind.

Supplementary information (3) (for Session 5)

How gender can be mainstreamed in key elements of organisational culture and systems

(This is not a handout)

Leadership
Managers need to provide clear and committed leadership and guidance on the importance of integrating gender equality into all aspects of the programme and the organisation's ways of working. They need to be able to articulate clearly the relationship between gender inequality and poverty.

Staff composition and capacity
There needs to be a reasonable balance between female and male members of staff at each level of the organisation, although the most important thing is that both men and women at all levels have the capacity required to integrate gender equality effectively into their work, especially for understanding poverty with a gender lens.

Human-resources systems
*   **Selection:** Capacity for working in a gender-sensitive manner should be a key criterion for all programme management and co-ordination posts. Interviews should include a question to assess the applicant's capacity for doing so.
*   **Induction:** All induction procedures should include an introduction to the organisation's approach to working on gender equality. Oxfam staff should be given a copy of Oxfam GB's Gender Policy, basic information on how Oxfam works on gender, basic bibliographic references, and useful Internet addresses.
*   **Performance management:** Working in a gender-sensitive manner, or towards the achievement of gender equality, should be part of the objectives of all programme staff.
*   **Code of conduct:** All Oxfam staff must be aware of the contents of the Code of Conduct, should sign it on starting work with Oxfam, and should abide by its contents. (See the Pick-up-and-Go course on Preventing Sexual Exploitation and Abuse, in this pack.)

Knowledge management and development
Good practice on gender mainstreaming should be shared across the programme.

Slide 1

Mainstreaming Gender Equality

Photo: Howard Davies

PICK–UP–AND–GO

Workshop objectives

■ **Know:** The key aspects of mainstreaming gender equality in programmes and organisational culture.

■ **Feel:** Motivated to ensure that gender equality is mainstreamed in the work that you support, and committed to challenge gender-based discrimination wherever it is found.

■ **Do:** Use a case study to practise mainstreaming gender equality in a project.

PICK–UP–AND–GO

Slide 2

Suggested ground rules

Participants should:

. Contribute their own examples and ideas.

. Listen to and respect the opinions of other learners.

. Respect other learners' right to confidentiality.

. Be present throughout the day.

Slide 3

PICK–UP–AND–GO

Pick-up-and-Go Training Pack • Mainstreaming Gender Equality in NGOs • Slides

Which project is gender-mainstreamed?....

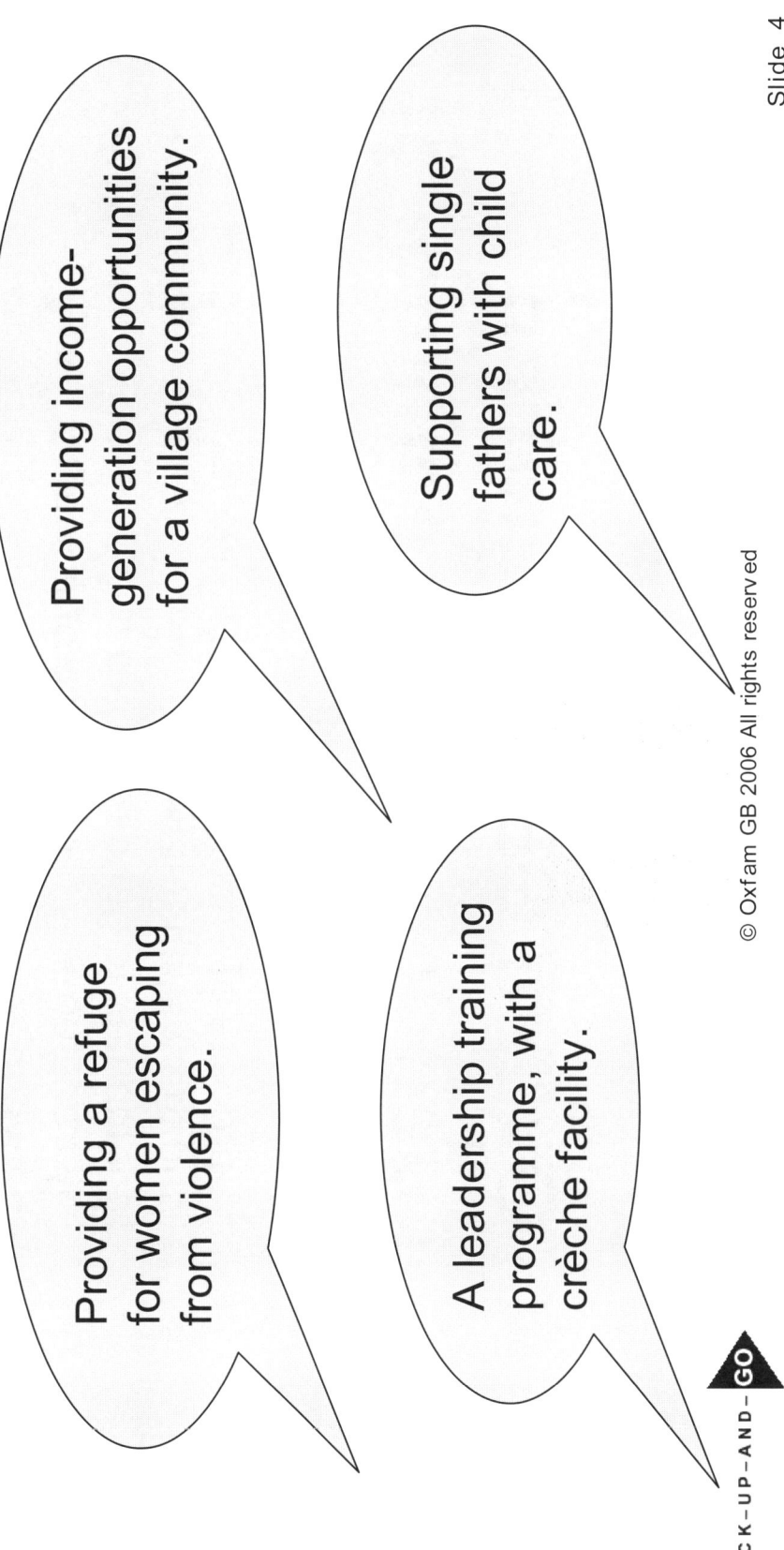

Providing income-generation opportunities for a village community.

Supporting single fathers with child care.

Providing a refuge for women escaping from violence.

A leadership training programme, with a crèche facility.

Slide 4

PICK–UP–AND–GO

Oxfam GB's definition of gender mainstreaming:

- A process of ensuring that all its work, and the way that it is done, contributes to gender equality by transforming the balance of power between women and men.

PICK–UP–AND–GO

Slide 5

Oxfam is mainstreaming gender equality into ....

The Programme

The Organisation

PICK–UP–AND–GO

Slide 6

Pick-up-and-Go Training Pack • Mainstreaming Gender Equality in NGOs • Slides

Oxfam GB integrates gender equality into its programme in two main ways:

By supporting projects specifically aimed at gender equity. ('SCO 5')

By addressing gender inequality in all Strategic Change Objectives

Slide 7

PICK–UP–AND–GO

103

SCO 5: The Right to Equity: Gender and Diversity

Women and men will enjoy equal rights

This work includes:

- focused support in 10 countries on gender mainstreaming

- intensive research in 5 countries on the impact of gender-equality mainstreaming

- a South Asia programme on ending violence against women – including a regional campaign

PICK–UP–AND–GO

Slide 8

Pick-up-and-Go Training Pack • Mainstreaming Gender Equality in NGOs • Slides

Simplified programme/ project management cycle

Needs-assessment (humanitarian)

Situation analysis

Planning, designing, redesigning

Partner appraisal

Monitoring, evaluation, impact assessment

Implementation

Slide 9

PICK–UP–AND–GO

105

Incorporating gender equality into Programme Implementation Plans (PIPs)

Poverty and policy analysis with gender awareness

Gender-aware
- Changes in policy, practice, ideas, beliefs
- Strategies
- Outcomes
- Impact

Slide 10

PICK–UP–AND–GO

Definition of gender analysis:
viewing poverty through a gender lens

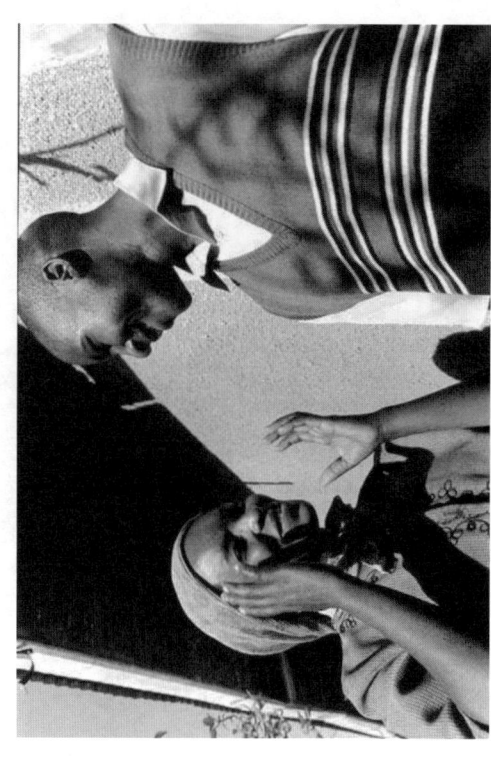

Photo: Geoff Sayer

- Examines how women and men relate to each other, and the inequalities of that relationship.

- Focuses on what disadvantaged women themselves identify as their concerns.

PICK–UP–AND–GO

Slide 11

Pick-up-and-Go Training Pack • Mainstreaming Gender Equality in NGOs • Slides

Slide 12

Gender analysis – basic questions

- **Who *does what?***
- **Who *has what?***
- **Who *decides?***
- **Who *gains? Who loses?***

PICK–UP–AND–GO

Pick-up-and-Go Training Pack • Mainstreaming Gender Equality in NGOs • Slides

Capacities and Vulnerabilities Framework

	Capacities		Vulnerabilities	
	Female	Male	Female	Male
Physical/ Material				
Social/ Organisational				
Motivational/ Attitudinal				

Slide 13

PICK-UP-AND-GO

Oxfam GB is mainstreaming gender equality into ....

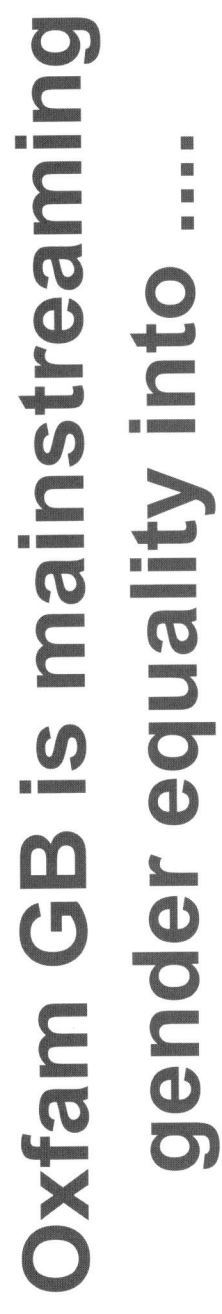

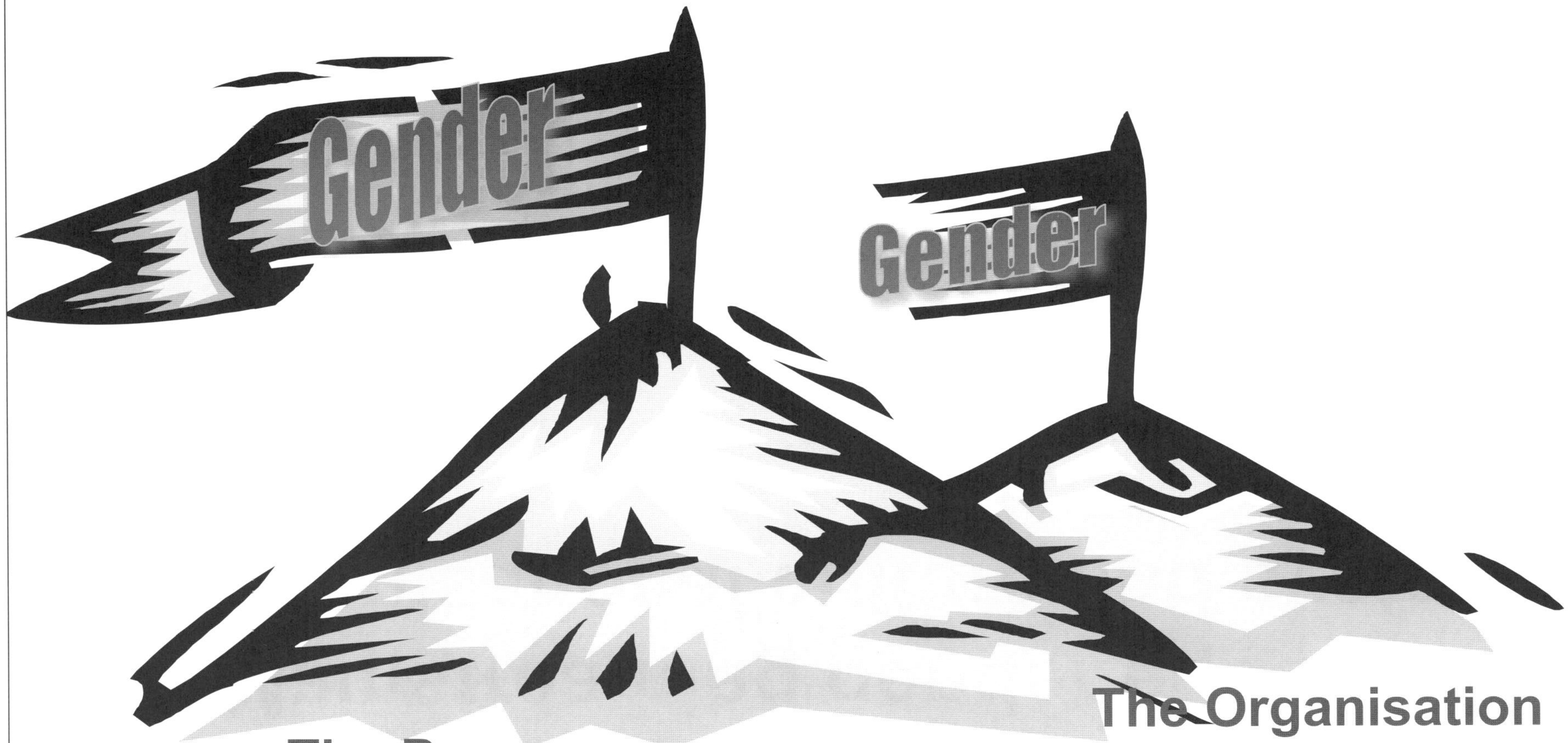

Gender
Gender
The Programme
The Organisation

PICK-UP-AND-GO

Slide 14

Pick-up-and-Go Training Pack • Mainstreaming Gender Equality in NGOs • Slides

Mainstreaming gender equality in organisational culture and systems

Leadership

Staff composition and capacity

Human-resources systems – Selection, induction, performance management, code of conduct

Knowledge management and development

PICK–UP–AND–GO

Slide 15

Preventing Sexual Exploitation and Abuse

A Training Course for All Staff

2 hours

Written by Yoma Winder
(Oxfam GB Humanitarian Programme Adviser)
with help, support, and contributions from many staff of Oxfam GB
around the world

Preventing Sexual Exploitation and Abuse

A Training Course for All Staff

Contents

Facilitator's notes

Handouts

Flipcharts 1–5   134

Supplementary information for facilitator

Facilitator's notes

Introduction

Information for workshop managers
Module length 2 hours
Facilitation skills • This module requires presentation skills and the management of facilitated discussion. • The level of facilitation skills required for this course will be determined by the degree of behavioural change that the workshop is required to deliver. • In Oxfam workshops, participants will ask questions about the Oxfam GB Code of Conduct and Sexual Conduct. The facilitator needs to be able to answer and debate these, and defend and promote Oxfam's positions, using the facilitator's notes and supporting documentation provided. • In Oxfam workshops, the facilitator must have had some degree of exposure to Oxfam's Code of Conduct, and experience of making management decisions on staff conduct. • Managers are responsible for ensuring that this workshop is delivered by a member of staff of sufficient capability.
Learners This module is intended for staff in non-management positions. Priority should be given to those who have any form of contact with beneficiaries.
Group size This course could be run for groups of 6 to 30. However, it is easier to facilitate learning with groups of 18 to 20. A group of this size generates the maximum amount of discussion among participants, and therefore maximum learning.

Information for facilitators
Room This module requires space for the whole group to be working together in a room – sitting in such a way that they can all see one another. It also requires sufficient space for the group to divide into smaller groups.
Equipment needed • One flipchart stand, paper, and pens (black or dark blue only to ensure visibility). • Post-it notes • Blu-tack
Preparation of material • Prepare flipcharts 1–5 in advance.

Preparation of the facilitator

The facilitator needs to read and become familiar with all the material, in addition to managing the preparation of the material and the room. Oxfam facilitators may seek advice from their regional focal point for sexual exploitation and abuse issues, line manager, or Human Resources team.

Supplementary material for the training session comes in two varieties. **S1 and S2** are essential material for running the training session, and the facilitator must be familiar and comfortable with their content. **S3, S4, and S5** (Oxfam GB policies and guidelines) are included as background information for facilitators, who are advised to read them before delivering the training. As an optional extra, Oxfam facilitators are recommended to read the following policies and guidelines on the Intranet:

- Anti-Harrassment Policy http://homepage.oxfam.org.uk/chr/polproc/7/harass.htm
- Behaviour at Work
  http://homepage.oxfam.org.uk/chr/polproc/10/behaviouratworkhomepage.htm
- Dealing with Problems at Work
  http://homepage.oxfam.org.uk/chr/polproc/7/problemsatwork.htm

Flipcharts 1–5 are intended to give an idea of how the actual flipcharts should look.

When making photocopies before the training session, DO NOT staple all the handouts together. Make sure they are stapled, separately, to be handed out at different times throughout the sessions.

Linked learning

Other Pick-up-and-Go packs:

- 'Preventing Sexual Exploitation and Abuse' – full-day and half-day training for managers.

For Oxfam GB staff:

- Ask your regional focal points, Human Resources team, or line manager for support before or after running the sessions.

Among your colleagues

It is every individual's responsibility to promote and uphold the principles that will reduce the likelihood of sexual exploitation and abuse being committed by staff. Please ensure that you take every opportunity to discuss this subject with your colleagues.

Translations

This module is currently available in English, Spanish, French, and Portuguese. If it would help learners, please feel free to translate all or part of it into additional languages – but please send a copy to Oxfam Publishing at Oxfam House.

Support and feedback

Please send questions, ideas, and feedback to learninternational@oxfam.org.uk

Workshop objectives

As a result of this workshop, employees of Oxfam GB will have an increased knowledge of and ability to comply with Oxfam GB's Internal Staff Code of Conduct. They will:

Know ...

- the principles that underpin Oxfam GB's Code of Conduct and the Guidelines for Sexual Conduct;
- their responsibilities as Oxfam staff members;
- the consequences of breaking rules or not fulfilling their responsibilities.

Feel ...

- confident about raising issues and reporting suspected incidents to the organisation;
- confident about what the organisation expects of them;
- warned about what will happen if they break the rules.

Do ...

- study cases of sexual exploitation and abuse and apply them to their own work.

Timetable

Start	Finish	Session
00.00	00.10	1. Introductions and objectives
00.10	00.25	2. Story telling
00.25	00.50	3. Rules and guidelines
00.50	00.60	4. Reporting unacceptable behaviour
01.00	01.50	5. Case studies
01.50	02.00	6. Close and evaluation

The timings for this event are shown as starting at 00.00. The actual timing will depend on the participants' normal working hours. This timetable can be divided into two sessions: input sessions first (1–4) and practice sessions second (5 and 6). This gives time for participants to absorb the information and discuss the implications, before they work on the case studies.

Note to the facilitator

The subjects of sexual exploitation and abuse, and the sexual conduct of staff, nearly always raise more questions than they answer. You should be aware that people feel strong emotions when their beliefs and personal values are challenged. Make sure that you read the supplementary documents 1 and 2 before delivering the session, and be sure that you can defend the positions taken in them.

Please remember, and emphasise to participants, that we run these workshops because we know that many beneficiaries are forced into sexual relations with humanitarian workers in order to obtain food, goods, or essential services for themselves and their families. Oxfam GB finds this intolerable and will do everything that it can to prevent it happening. Those found sexually exploiting or abusing beneficiaries will (subject to due process) be dismissed for gross misconduct.

The discussions during the day will raise many important issues, but you must move the course along and delay questions until the relevant session, when they might be covered anyway.

- Pay careful attention to the timings of the course and be prepared to chair the event. Remember that not every question can be asked or answered within the course of one day.
- Put a page of flipchart paper on the wall to 'park' questions that arise. This is a way of clearly acknowledging a question without having to answer it at that time – but if you have not answered all of the questions by the end of the course, you should clearly identify the means by which you will answer them (for example, by consulting an appropriate colleague and then sending the answer by email to all of the participants).
- In order to maintain the pace and energy of the course, you need to be very clear about timings and instructions. If you give 10 minutes for groups to do an exercise, after 5 minutes you should announce that 5 minutes remain; after 9 minutes, announce that one minute remains – and then finish after 10 minutes. You will find that groups often produce better results if they feel under a reasonable degree of pressure.

Session 1   Introduction and objectives

TOTAL TIME: 10 minutes

Purpose: by the end of this session, participants will know the aim of this workshop and know who is in the room.

Timing	What YOU do	What the LEARNERS do	Resources
00.00	• Introduce yourself. • Ask the participants to introduce themselves by telling the group their name, their job title, and the country or project area in which they work. Tell the participants that they will only have a very few minutes to do this.	• Ask questions if they need clarification. • Introduce themselves, but very briefly.	Name badges if appropriate
00.05	• Introduce the course objectives: show Flipchart 1 and attach it to the wall where it can be seen throughout all sessions. Read the objectives to participants and ask if they have any questions.	• Read the objectives thoroughly and ensure that they match their own understanding and expectation of the course.	Flipchart 1

Session 2   Story telling

Purpose: to demonstrate the extent and implications of the problem; to establish that some NGO staff commit abuse and exploitation, and that Oxfam GB will not tolerate this behaviour among its own staff.

Timing	What YOU do	What the LEARNERS do	Resources
00.10	• Tell the participants the following story. Guards at an NGO compound were allowing beneficiary families to enter the compound at night to collect water from the office tap. In exchange for this favour, they were forcing the younger women and girls to have sex with them. A complaint was eventually made by some of the women, and an investigation supported their complaint. The guards were suspended when the investigation began, and they were dismissed when the complaint was found to be true. They were not allowed to work their notice period, and they received no end-of-contract benefits.	• Listen carefully to the case studies. Think about what they mean – to themselves, their families, the people that they work with, their jobs. • Tell a story from their own experience (if they have one, and if they want to tell it). • Ask questions for clarification or quick comment.	'Parking' flipchart
00.15	• Ask the group if anyone has a similar story that they would like to share. • If not, tell them this one: an NGO project officer overseeing an education programme was proved, eventually, of raping not only teachers but also pupils. He was instantly dismissed, with no notice period and no end-of-contract benefits whatsoever. • Ask for comments on these stories. • Emphasise that the stories that you have told are real stories from real NGO staff – that sexual exploitation and abuse of beneficiaries really does happen. • If you have time, you can ask again if there is anybody who has a similar story that they want to share. If not, move on to the next session.		
00.25			

Session 3   Rules and guidelines

Purpose: to know what is and what is not allowed; and how and why Oxfam GB has made its rules and guidelines.

Timing	What YOU do	What the LEARNERS do	Resources
00.25	• Divide the group into small groups of 4 or 5. Give each group one piece of flipchart paper and a pen. • Put up Flipchart 2 and ask each group to write down what they know about the organisation's rules concerning sexual conduct. Tell them that they have only 10 minutes for this.	• Form small groups as requested. • Brainstorm and write down what they know about the organisation's rules for sexual conduct. • Choose one person to read and explain these to the whole group when asked. • Comment on what other groups have written. • Look closely at the rules that the organisation *does* have and comment on what they mean to them.	Flipchart paper Pens Handouts 1 and 2 Flipcharts 2 and 3
00.35	• Bring the group back together and ask one group after another to report what they have written down. • Ask other groups to comment on the answers. In particular, try to get other groups to say whether the 'rules' as written down are correct or not. • Give Handout 1 to all participants. Ask them to read it thoroughly and discuss it with their neighbour. • Stick Flipchart 3 on the wall and read through the two very simple rules. • Ask if Handout 1 and Flipchart 3 say the same thing. Discuss. NB At this stage you may need to start defending the organisation's position. Make sure that you have read through the supporting documentation thoroughly and are fully able to debate the issues. • Give out the Code of Conduct (Handout 2) and encourage participants to read it as soon as they can. The important bits are in **bold.** • Emphasise that they should contact their manager or their nearest Human Resources staff member if they feel any confusion or concern about the Code.		
00.50			

Session 4   Reporting unacceptable behaviour

TOTAL TIME: 10 minutes

Purpose: to consider and discuss reasons why staff might want to report unacceptable behaviour, and the procedures for doing it.

Timing	What YOU do	What the LEARNERS do	Resources
00.50	• Ask the group what the word 'whistle-blowing' means. (It is an English idiom meaning 'to report illegal or unacceptable behaviour'.) Ask if there is a local equivalent. Check this with others in the group, to ensure that the right word is being used! • Ask why people would want to whistle-blow. • Ask what the risks associated with whistle-blowing might be. • Explain Oxfam GB's whistle-blowing procedure. • Give a copy of Handout 3 to all participants. • Talk them through the really important bits of the document (genuine concern, confidentiality, correct procedure) and ask questions to check that they understand it. *Who can use this procedure?* *What should you use it for?* *To whom should worried members talk?* *To whom should they not talk?* *What will happen if the procedure is abused?* *etc ...*	• Try to translate the term 'whistle-blowing' into local languages. • Answer questions as asked, and debate with other learners as appropriate. • Read the handout. • Answer questions about the whistle-blowing procedure.	Handout 3
01.00			

Session 5   Case studies

TOTAL TIME: 50 minutes

Purpose: To use information from previous sessions to practise and role-play some real-life case studies. To discuss, debate, and learn from others what is expected of them in terms of their behaviour and their responsibilities.

Timing	What YOU do	What the LEARNERS do	Resources
01.00	• Divide participants into three groups (regardless of the number of total participants). • Each group will work on a different case study – three groups, three case studies. Give a copy of Handout 4 to each participant and make it clear which group must work on which case study. Ensure that each group has at least one piece of flipchart paper. NB It is normally OK to use the same case studies that were used in the opening session, because they will not yet have been discussed in depth. There are more case studies provided than you will probably have time to use, so feel free to 'mix and match' them as you like.	• Read the case study closely. • Discuss it with other members of their small group. • Answer the questions that follow the case study. • Write these answers up and be prepared to explain and defend them to the whole group. • Make sure that they finish the exercise within the 20-minute time limit. • Listen carefully to others' answers and ask for clarification of anything that they do not understand.	Handout 4 Flipchart paper
01.05	• Tell them they have only 15 minutes to read the case study, discuss it, and answer the questions that it poses. Ask them to write their answers on a sheet of flipchart paper. • Move round the groups and encourage them to look at all aspects of the case study and all angles from which it could be viewed. • Tell the participants when they have only 5 minutes left.		
01.20	• Bring the small groups back together and ask each in turn to present their answers. • Discuss the answers as a large group and ensure that the 'right' answers are clear to all at the end. NB Make sure that you have read supplementary documents 1 and 2 before you present this session. It is very important for you to be familiar with the 'right' answers to many of the questions that people will ask.		
01.50			

Session 6   Close and evaluation

Timing	What YOU do	What the LEARNERS do	Resources
01.50	• Refer back to the flipchart on which the course objectives were written. Ask participants whether they feel that they have met the objectives.	▪ Question whether they really feel that they are happy and confident that the original objectives have been met.	Flipcharts 4 and 5
01.55	• Allow five minutes to discuss any outstanding queries and requests for clarification.	▪ Raise any outstanding queries.	
	• Look at the 'parking' flipchart and see if any of the questions there can now be answered.	▪ Complete the evaluation flipcharts.	
02.00	• Stick the two evaluation flipcharts up on the wall. Ask participants to consider the two questions, and mark an x on the flipchart to indicate the extent to which they agree with the statement.		

Handout 1
Sexual Conduct Guidelines from Oxfam GB's Code of Conduct

Oxfam's Code of Conduct provides guidelines for the way Oxfam intends its staff to behave. The guidelines are necessarily broad, covering all aspects of behaviour, use of equipment, and guidance on relationships with others at many levels and in many situations.

The Code draws on and makes reference to many of Oxfam's policies (use of computers, harassment, etc.) but there is no policy on sexual conduct or child protection. Below you will find a distillation of how Oxfam requires its staff to behave in this regard.

The underlying, **non-negotiable** principles that we expect to govern your behaviour and that of those around you are the following:

- No exploitation or relationships that are exploitative as a result of your position within Oxfam.
- No actions that bring the organisation into disrepute.

Therefore …

- No sexual contact at all with anybody under the age of 18 (because it is exploitative by nature).
- No sexual contact at all with beneficiaries (because it is potentially exploitative by nature).

To clarify:

- You must not demand or accept sex or sexual contact in return for goods or services from you or Oxfam.

Essential warning:

- It is your duty and responsibility to report, via the systems that exist, behaviour that you feel is not in accordance with the above requirements.
- It is also your responsibility to actively promote and maintain an atmosphere or environment in which staff feel that they can and will live up to the expectations clarified above.

Handout 2
Oxfam GB Code of Conduct

As an Oxfam GB staff member, you are required to abide by the organisation's policies and procedures, the terms and conditions of your employment (as outlined in your employment contract), and to ensure that your conduct is in keeping with the organisation's beliefs, values, and aims.

The aim of this Code of Conduct is to give you guidance regarding the key issues that you need to be aware of as an Oxfam GB staff member, and the standards by which you may need to behave in certain circumstances. The Code applies to all Oxfam GB staff, regardless of location, and in accepting appointment, you undertake to discharge your duties and to regulate your conduct in line with the requirements of this Code. The Code is designed for your guidance and protection, although a breach may result in disciplinary action (including dismissal in some instances) and, in some cases, may lead to criminal prosecution.

While we recognise that local laws and cultures differ considerably from one country to another, Oxfam GB is a British-based International NGO, and therefore the Code of Conduct is based on European and international legal standards, as well as being written to reflect the organisation's fundamental beliefs and values (as outlined below), to support its mission to work with others to overcome poverty and suffering and its commitment to ensuring that staff members avoid using possible unequal power relationships for their own benefit.

Oxfam GB – mission, beliefs, and values

Oxfam GB's purpose	-	To work with others to overcome poverty and suffering.
GB's beliefs	-	The lives of all human beings are of equal value.
		In a world rich in resources, poverty is an injustice, which must be overcome.
		Poverty makes people more vulnerable to conflict and natural calamity; much of this suffering can be prevented and must be relieved.
		People's vulnerability to poverty and suffering is increased by unequal power relations based on, for example, gender, race, class, caste, and disability; women, who make up the majority of the world's poor, are especially disadvantaged.
		Working together we can build a just and safer world, in which people take control over their own lives and enjoy their basic rights.
		To overcome poverty and suffering involves changing unjust policies and practices, nationally and internationally, as well as working closely with people in poverty.
Oxfam GB's anti-harassment policy	-	Oxfam GB views all forms of harassment as incompatible with its aims and beliefs in the dignity of all people, and undermining to its vision of equal opportunities. Consequently, Oxfam GB will not tolerate the harassment of staff, volunteers, contractors, partner organisations, beneficiaries, or any others.

Code of conduct – standards

As a staff member of Oxfam GB, I will:

1. **Be responsible for the use of information and resources to which I have access by reason of my employment with Oxfam GB.**
   - I will ensure that I use Oxfam GB information, funds, and resources entrusted to me in a responsible manner and will account for all money and property, following the appropriate policy and procedural requirements. Resources and property include
        Oxfam GB vehicles
        Telephones, photocopiers, fax machines, and stationery
        Other office equipment or equipment/resources belonging to Oxfam GB
        Computers, including the use of email, internet, and intranet
        Oxfam GB accommodation (including Oxfam housing in international locations)

2. **Ensure safety, health, and welfare of all Oxfam GB staff members, volunteers, and contractors.**
   - I will adhere to all legal and organisational health and safety requirements in force at the location of my work.
   - I will comply with any local security guidelines and be pro-active in informing management of any necessary changes to such guidelines.
   - I will behave in such a way as to avoid any unnecessary risk to the safety, health, and welfare of myself and others, including partner organisations and beneficiaries.

3. **Ensure that my personal and professional conduct is, and is seen to be, of the highest standards and in keeping with Oxfam GB's beliefs, values, and aims.**
   - I will treat all people fairly and with respect and dignity.
   - When working in an international context or travelling internationally on behalf of Oxfam GB, I will observe all local laws and be sensitive to local customs.
   - I will not work under the influence of alcohol or use, or be in possession of, illegal substances on Oxfam GB premises or accommodation.
   - I will seek to ensure that my sexual conduct does not bring Oxfam GB into any ill repute and does not affect or undermine my ability to undertake the role for which I am employed.
   - I will not enter into commercial sex transactions with beneficiaries. For the purpose of this Code of Conduct, a transaction is classed as any exchange of money, goods, services, or favours with any other person.

4. **Perform my duties and conduct my private life in a manner that avoids possible conflicts of interest with the work of Oxfam GB and my work as a staff member of the organisation.**
   - I will declare any financial, personal, family (or close intimate relationship) interest in matters of official business which may affect the work of Oxfam GB, e.g. contract for goods/services, employment or promotion within Oxfam GB, partner organisations, civil authorities, beneficiary groups.
   - I will behave in a manner that does not undermine national or international perceptions of Oxfam GB's impartiality.
   - I will seek permission before agreeing to being nominated as a prospective candidate or other official role for any political party.
   - I will not accept any additional employment or consultancy work outside Oxfam GB without prior permission from management.
   - I will not accept significant gifts or any remuneration from governments, beneficiaries, donors, suppliers, and other persons which have been offered to me as a result of my employment with Oxfam GB.
   - I will not abuse my position as an Oxfam GB staff member by requesting any service or favour from others in return for assistance by Oxfam GB.

5. **Avoid involvement in any criminal activities, activities that contravene human rights, or those that compromise the work of Oxfam GB.**
   - I will contribute to combating all forms of illegal activities.
   - I will notify Oxfam GB of any unspent criminal convictions or charges prior to employment.
   - I will also notify the organisation if I face any criminal charges during my employment.
   - I will not engage in sexual behaviour with children under the age of 18, regardless of local custom.
   - I will not abuse or exploit children under the age of 18 in any way and will report any such behaviour of others to my line management.

6. **Refrain from any form of harassment, discrimination, physical or verbal abuse, intimidation or exploitation.**
   - I will fully abide with the requirements of Oxfam GB's policies on equal opportunities, diversity, and anti-harassment.
   - I will never engage in any exploitative, abusive, or corrupt relationships.

I have read carefully and understand the Oxfam GB Code of Conduct and hereby agree to abide by its requirements and commit myself to upholding the standards of conduct required to support Oxfam GB's aims, values and beliefs.

Name

Signature   Date

Application of the code of conduct

The Code of Conduct is intended to serve as a guide for all Oxfam GB staff in making decisions in their professional lives and, at times, in their private lives. By following this Code of Conduct, it is intended that all staff will contribute to strengthening the professionalism and impact of the work of Oxfam GB.

The Code of Conduct forms part of the terms and conditions of employment of all staff. Further information and detail on specific aspects of this Code can also be found in 'Behaviour at Work' in Oxfam GB's Policies and Procedures.

1. All staff will be given a copy of this Code of Conduct and be required to familiarise themselves with its requirements, by reading and discussing the Code with their manager or colleagues.
2. All staff will be required to confirm this by signing their agreement to the Code of Conduct and by keeping a copy. A further copy of the signed agreement will be kept on the staff member's personal file.
3. Further information on the provisions within the Code can be found in Oxfam GB's policies, procedures and guidelines. Staff can also seek further clarification from their manager or a member of the Human Resources team.
4. For staff relocating to another country of work, guidance will also be given in relation to local specific customs and legal requirements, in order to inform the behaviour that they will be expected to adopt.
5. Further guidance and information will also be distributed to each office and work place and may also be found in related documents (e.g. Local Security Guidelines).
6. Managers have a responsibility to ensure that all staff, including newly recruited staff, are provided with a copy of the Code of Conduct, understand its provisions clearly, and sign their agreements to its terms.
7. Managers also have a particular responsibility to uphold the standards of conduct and to set an example.
8. In the recruitment and selection of staff, managers should seek to ensure that candidates selected support the beliefs and values of Oxfam GB and do not have a work history that contravenes the requirements of this Code.
9. Any staff member who has concerns about the behaviour of another staff member should raise these with the appropriate line manager. Any concerns will be treated with urgency, consideration and discretion.
10. Any breaches of the requirements of this Code of Conduct will be subject to investigation and possible disciplinary action in line with Oxfam GB's disciplinary procedure.

Handout 3
Disclosure of Malpractice in the Workplace (Worldwide)

Policy

Oxfam GB believes that good communications between staff and volunteers at all levels throughout the organisation promote better business practice. Staff and volunteers are encouraged to raise genuine concerns about malpractice in the workplace, without fear of reprisals, and Oxfam GB will protect them from victimisation and dismissal.

Scope: All Oxfam GB staff and volunteers.

Procedures

Oxfam GB has introduced these procedures to enable staff and volunteers to raise or disclose concerns at an early stage and in the right way. They apply in all cases where there are genuine concerns about malpractice in the workplace, regardless of where this may be and whether the information involved is confidential or not.

If an individual raises a genuine concern and is acting in good faith, even if it is later discovered that he or she is mistaken, under this policy they will not be at risk of losing their job or suffering any form of retribution as a result. This assurance will not be extended to an individual who maliciously raises a matter they know to be untrue or who is involved in any way in the malpractice.

Raising a concern

Any member of staff or volunteer who genuinely believes that the actions of someone working for Oxfam GB could lead to, or have resulted in:

- a criminal offence;
- a failure to comply with any legal obligations;
- a miscarriage of justice
- danger to the health and safety of any individual;
- damage to the environment; or
- the deliberate concealment of information which may lead to any of the matters listed above

should raise the matter with their line manager. Where this is not appropriate because the line manager is involved in the alleged malpractice in some way, the matter should be raised with the line manager's manager and brought to the attention of the Head of the Divisional/Regional Human Resources team. This may be done orally or in writing and should include full details and, if possible, supporting evidence.

Confidentiality

It is recognised that the individual may want to raise a concern in confidence under this policy. If the individual asks for his or her identity to be kept confidential, it will not be disclosed without his or her consent. However, if it is not possible to resolve the concern without revealing the individual's identity, the manager will discuss the implications with the individual, and a decision not to proceed with the investigation may need to be made. In order to avoid hindering an investigation into malpractice, anonymous disclosures are strongly discouraged.

(Note to workshop participants: this is just a small part of the 'Disclosure of Malpractice in the Workplace' document. Request the full document from the facilitator if you are interested.)

Handout 4
Case studies

The following case studies are fictional, but each one is based on elements of fact.

Case Study 1: Girls as gifts

During field visits at a particular location, it was customary for chiefs to offer young girls in the village as gifts to the staff of NGO X to thank them for the partnership with the NGO. This happened for many years before any staff objected or raised the issue. One day this happened to an honest staff member, who then reported it to senior management. It turned out to be a regular occurrence. The case was even more serious because nearly all the girls offered were under 18.

What is wrong with this? Who is in the wrong? What should the 'honest' staff member say to the chief? What should the NGO do next? Should the police be involved?

Case Study 2: Extra food for a relationship

Josie is an adolescent girl living in a camp. Samuel, one of Oxfam's food distribution staff, has offered to give her a little extra food during distributions if she will be his 'special friend'. She agrees willingly. Both of them agree to start a sexual relationship, and neither of them thinks there is anything wrong. Josie hopes that the relationship will be a passport to a new life out of the camp. Samuel does nothing to discourage these hopes.

Who is in the right? Who is in the wrong? As Samuel's manager, what actions would you take? What actions could you take to reduce the likelihood of this happening again?

Case Study 3: Car rides for sex

Joey is a local driver hired by Oxfam GB to transport relief items from the warehouse to camps, where they are distributed. On one of his trips he recognises a 15-year-old girl walking along the side of the road and gives her a lift back to the camp. Since then, to impress her and win her over, he frequently offers to drive her wherever she is going and sometimes gives her small items from the relief packages in his truck, which he thinks that she and her family could use. The last time he drove her home, she invited him inside the house to meet her family; afterwards they had sex. The family is pleased that she has a relationship with an NGO worker.

Who is in the right? Who is in the wrong? What would you do if you were Joey's colleague? What messages would you want to give to the rest of your team? How would you do this?

Case Study 4: Living in the camps

Staff working on a fast-paced, first-phase emergency response programme are travelling at least 4 hours a day to reach the camps in which they are delivering an integrated water and sanitation programme. The travelling, they feel, is reducing their effectiveness to an unacceptable level. Their programme co-ordinator, based several hundred km away in the provincial capital, receives a formal request from the team to move their living quarters from the small and inhospitable town where they currently live to the largest, and most central, of the refugee camps. This, they feel, will make them safer, less tired, and far more effective in their jobs.

If you were the programme coordinator, what would your response and your actions be?

Case study 5: Misuse of Oxfam material

1a   First scenario

A local staff member has admitted accessing pornographic websites via an Oxfam laptop. The staff member is known to have received a full and correct induction which included a good briefing on the Code of Conduct, and illegal/illicit use of Oxfam's equipment had been explained and discussed in detail.

1b   Second scenario

A local staff member has admitted accessing pornographic websites via an Oxfam laptop. The staff member has not had a briefing by either the line manager or Human Resources.

1c   Third scenario

A local staff member has admitted accessing pornographic websites on an Oxfam computer. His defence (which he doesn't think he really needs) is that it is culturally acceptable in his country (and the country in which he is based) to do this and he doesn't understand why Oxfam finds fault with this. As his manager, you cannot be sure that he has received a full briefing on Oxfam's Code of Conduct.

What would be your response in each of the cases outlined above?

Flipchart 1

As a result of this workshop,
employees of Oxfam GB
will have a greater knowledge of,
and ability to comply with,
Oxfam GB's internal Staff Code of
Conduct.

Flipchart 2

In your small groups, write down
on the flipchart paper
your understanding of your
organisation's rules on the
sexual conduct of all staff.

Flipchart 3

No sexual contact at all
with anybody under the age of 18
(because it is exploitative by nature).

No commercial or transactional sex
with beneficiaries
(because it is exploitative by nature).

Flipchart 4

How well do you think you understand
what is meant by
'unacceptable behaviour'?

Well .... Not well

Flipchart 5

How well do you think you know
what actions you should take
if your friends or colleagues
are behaving unacceptably?

Well .... Not well

Supplementary information (1)
Answers to case studies
(Not a handout – intended for the facilitator only)

Case Study 1

Accepting gifts, goods, or services in return for help and support from Oxfam GB breaks our Code of Conduct, which states very clearly that staff must not do this. It therefore follows that if staff do accept gifts, goods or services, disciplinary action will immediately result.

Beneficiaries should get what they need without having to pay, in any way. Accepting gifts (of any nature) compromises the individual and Oxfam and is considered a conflict of interest. If you accept gifts from beneficiaries, it is impossible to know whether they have been chosen as beneficiaries because they need Oxfam's assistance or because they have paid you to become a beneficiary. This is an impossible and unacceptable position in which to put Oxfam or a beneficiary.

If any of the girls who were offered to Oxfam GB staff were under 18, this breaks our Code of Conduct in a second way. We judge that girls under the age of 18 are still children and, as such, are not to be put in a position where they must decide whether to start a sexual relationship with anybody. This rule holds true even if the law of the land is different, and even if the Oxfam staff member does not know the age of the girl. Having sex with a girl under 18 is likely to result in immediate dismissal.

In this case, the Oxfam staff member is in the wrong. But hardly anybody is in the right (although, in most cases the girls will be virtually blameless because they are unlikely to have been consulted!). Oxfam should launch investigative and disciplinary proceedings against any staff member who is thought to have accepted a girl while visiting this village. In addition, further information about the Code of Conduct and Guidelines for Sexual Conduct must be disseminated immediately. A visit should be made to the village to explain why Oxfam GB will no longer accept their kind gifts. It would be good to ask community members to tell Oxfam GB if its staff members continue to behave wrongly.

Case Study 2

Samuel is exploiting Josie and giving Oxfam GB property away in order to have a relationship. Josie is a beneficiary and she has the right to expect that Oxfam staff will exercise full duty of care for her. In addition, Samuel is stealing from Oxfam. Both these acts contravene Oxfam's Code of Conduct; exploitation and stealing are both acts of gross misconduct, and Samuel should expect to be dismissed. Josie may well be under 18, a fact which will make the gravity of Samuel's case even more severe.

As his manager, you will need to start investigative and disciplinary proceedings. More information on what Oxfam GB expects from its staff members must be given to all staff. In addition it would be very useful to talk with beneficiaries and their leaders to explain to them what they can and cannot expect from Oxfam GB staff. It is also important to set up a system whereby you and your team can hear the complaints of beneficiaries and respond to them.

Case Study 3

Joey is in the wrong, already, for several reasons:

- He should not be giving lifts to somebody who is not a member of Oxfam's staff and who is not authorised to travel in an Oxfam vehicle. This warrants a stern warning, if not a disciplinary procedure.
- He should not be giving her 'gifts' that are not his to give, even if he has asked for nothing in return. This warrants a stern warning, if not a disciplinary procedure.
- If he starts a relationship with her, he will be guilty of exploitation – both by sleeping with an underage girl and by exchanging goods for sexual contact. This is gross misconduct, and formal disciplinary procedures should be immediately started and Joey should be suspended. If the case is proved, he will then immediately lose his job.

In all likelihood, many managers would feel the need (and under most circumstances would be advised) to dismiss Joey (with due process) for the first two of these offences and not merely the last one.

Case Study 4

You should give a definite 'no' to the team. Immediately. This is for a number of reasons, including the following:

- Security in the camps is likely to be very poor and there is often little action that aid workers can take to improve matters.
- As aid workers living in the camp, they will get no peace whatsoever: they will receive requests for support and assistance continually and will find it almost impossible to protect themselves against this.
- They will become, inevitably, a target for those seeking a way out of the camp. Offers of sexual favours will become difficult to ignore. Behaving in the fair and transparent way that Oxfam GB expects will become increasingly difficult.
- The level of HIV infection is bound to be very high among the camp population. Any sexual relations that might result would put all concerned at extreme risk.
- The presence of relatively well-paid aid workers with seemingly endless resources will result in jealousy and poor perception of the workers and/or organisation involved, which may well lead to difficulties in programme implementation.

Case Study 5
First scenario
From Oxfam GB's policy on Internet use:

'The following are some examples of misuse which would be classified as acts of gross misconduct under the disciplinary procedures and as such may result in summary dismissal, without prior warning and notice. The list is not exhaustive:

- violating the privacy of other users;

- corrupting or destroy other users' data or disrupting their work;

- creating, accessing or displaying any criminal, offensive, obscene or indecent images, data or other material.'

Therefore this is an act that deserves sanction through the disciplinary procedures. The staff member has broken the terms of his contract and has not followed Oxfam GB's procedures, instructions, and policy as set out in the Internet Use Policy. Decisions about what sanction(s) to apply are left to the line manager, but it is clear that at the very least this behaviour is a Performance Management issue. Some staff members who access pornographic websites have been dismissed for gross misconduct.

In addition the manager(s) concerned should take the opportunity of convening a staff meeting or similar to explain the Internal Code and the guidance on Sexual Conduct and maybe carry out some work on case studies appropriate to the context.

Second scenario
This is still a disciplinary offence, because it contravenes the policy quoted above. The offending staff member probably deserves a formal, verbal warning with a note of the fact added to their file. In addition, the staff member's manager (because he or she has not ensured that the code of conduct was given to the employee) should be held responsible for this transgression, and a formal, verbal warning should probably be issued to them also; their inability to carry out adequate inductions should become a performance-management issue.

The staff member must immediately receive a copy of the Code of Conduct and should be given training on it and the responsibility that it requires of him. The staff member's manager must be made aware of his or her responsibility to promote and maintain an atmosphere in which staff feel they can and will live up to Oxfam's guidelines and rulings on sexual abuse and exploitation and sexual conduct. The manager's willingness and ability to do this is a performance-management issue and should be closely monitored.

Every effort must be made to reinforce key messages about Oxfam's rules on the use of equipment and the responsibility of all to promote and maintain an atmosphere where staff can and will uphold the Internal Code.

Third scenario
As with the above answer, a formal, verbal warning would probably be the most appropriate primary response – both for the staff member concerned and for the manager (with notes added to their files to document the fact that this has been done). However, in addition, it is obvious that some work needs to be done with the staff member to help him to understand, and live up to, Oxfam GB's Internal Code of Conduct and guidelines for sexual conduct.

It must be clear to all staff, whatever their level, that Oxfam GB is fully aware that the global 'Oxfam' culture that we are promoting is sometimes not in accordance with local culture. In all circumstances, Oxfam GB culture should take precedence over local culture – always.

It would probably be a good idea to carry out training/reminder sessions with all staff at an opportune time. The judgements that Oxfam GB has made on what is acceptable and what is not acceptable may differ quite radically from the local 'norm'. Although these differences are interesting, and much can be learned from debating them, the fact is that Oxfam GB has thought long and hard and has produced rules and guidelines that it feels are necessary and appropriate. Staff members must promote and maintain these rules and guidelines; or they and their managers should recognise that they are in the wrong organisation, and they need to leave.

Supplementary information (2)
Frequently asked questions: some thoughts

(Not a handout – for the facilitator only)

'But in my country the age of consent is lower than 18, and it is culturally acceptable to marry girls as young as 15.'
In many countries this **is** the case. But the Convention on the Rights of the Child, to which virtually all countries are signatory, states that childhood should continue up to the age of 18. This is Oxfam GB's policy. We will help staff to live up to it.

'My colleague X has been married for the last two years to somebody who is now only 16. Are you going to dismiss him?'
It is unlikely that this will be legally possible. But, now that we have introduced this clear new policy, we will not tolerate new staff or old staff starting a relationship with a child. In some countries we will be able to ask about marital status at interview, in others we will not: but we will make every effort to find out. Our recruitment procedures are about to become much more robust, to enable us to offer maximum protection to people in our care. Oxfam's approach from now on is one of deterrence and detection: we will advertise broadly and clearly our position in relation to the protection of children, and then we will be rigorous in following up references, employment history, and criminal records where possible. In addition, we will be increasing the level of attention that we pay to these issues, and managers and staff alike will be more confident and competent to make the environment in which we work safe for vulnerable people.

'Prostitution is legal in this country. Many people pay for sex with sex workers, there is little stigma attached.'
Yes we know. We are not banning the use of sex workers, but we are **strongly** recommending people to avoid using them, for many reasons. First of all there is the fundamental principle that any transaction of this sort is the result of an unequal power dynamic and is therefore exploitative. There is every possibility that indulging in transactional sex will bring Oxfam GB into disrepute, and there is often the distinct possibility that it will increase security risks for individuals and Oxfam alike. There is every chance that it will also have direct security implications for the sex workers themselves.

'If Oxfam takes such a strong stance on gender equity, why hasn't it banned the use of sex workers?'
No, we haven't banned the use of prostitutes, but we **strongly** discourage it. We don't ban it, because we cannot infringe on people's civil liberties, and we know it would be impractical to think we could enforce a total ban. We also, in a number of countries, support partner organisations that work with sex workers to ensure their basic rights; so we are definitely not in any position to tell sex workers how to live their lives.

'You might think that my relationship is exploitative, but it doesn't feel like that to me, or to my partner. You are not in a position to pass judgement.'
This might be true. But if this relationship is with a minor or a beneficiary, then our fundamental principles tell us that this relationship is, by its very nature, exploitative and not something that Oxfam will condone. Indeed, disciplinary action can and should result immediately.

If the relationship is not with a minor or a beneficiary, there is less justification for Oxfam GB to intervene or pass judgement. But if you, as a manager, feel that there is something exploitative about the relationship, then you are probably right. Therefore it is worth investigating.

'If we are so keen to protect children, why don't we check new recruits more rigorously when they start work for Oxfam?'

We realise that we need to do more, and work is already underway to fill the gap. We are taking advice from other specialist agencies in the field, and the new procedures that we draw up will emphasise our absolute duty of care to those in our charge, and also the fact that more robust procedures will require more resources.

'Yes, I am having a relationship with a beneficiary but I haven't given them anything in exchange, so I am not exploiting the power that I have or the position that I hold within Oxfam.'

Maybe not. But others will either not see this or not recognise it. So, in order not to risk tarnishing Oxfam GB's reputation, we are saying that sexual relationships with beneficiaries are unacceptable. It is as much the *potential* for abuse, in addition to abuse itself, that we need to guard against.

'I know many Oxfam GB staff who are having relationships within their management line. What does Oxfam feel about this, and what is the guidance to me, or others, if we find ourselves in this situation?'

Oxfam GB does not forbid relationships within the management line, but it does insist upon transparency. If you are having a relationship with somebody whom you manage, it is **your** responsibility to let **your** manager know. It is then up to the manager (and maybe others) to decide whether the relationship could result in a potential conflict of interest in any way. In all such cases, Oxfam GB needs to find an alternative so that you are not responsible for the Performance Management of your partner.

'The Oxfam Code is vague on sexual conduct and is not prescriptive enough to help managers.'

It is not so much vague as rather broad. In addition we don't have a policy on sexual conduct at present, so we can't refer you to it for further clarity and guidance. What we do have are the 'Sexual Conduct Guidelines', information, and training packs, and soon Sexual Exploitation Focal Points will be appointed in each region and project areas as appropriate. In the meantime please feel free to contact your closest Human Resources team or sexual exploitation focal point.

Supplementary information (3)
Oxfam GB Policy on Gender Equity

(Not a handout – for the facilitator only)

Oxfam's mission is to work with others to overcome poverty and suffering.

People experience poverty when they are denied the right to livelihoods, water, education and health, protection and security, a voice in public life, or freedom from discrimination. Oxfam's definition of poverty goes beyond the purely economic to encompass capabilities, powerlessness and inequality.

Women often have less recourse than men to legal recognition and protection, as well as lower access to public knowledge and information, and less decision-making power both within and outside the home. Women in many parts of the world frequently have little control over fertility, sexuality and marital choices. This systematic discrimination reduces women's public participation, often increases their vulnerability to poverty, violence and HIV, and results in women representing a disproportionate percentage of the poor population of the world.

Gender equality gives women and men the same entitlements to all aspects of human development, including economic, social, cultural, civil and political rights; the same level of respect; the same opportunities to make choices; and the same level of power to shape the outcomes of these choices.[1]

This policy represents our organisational commitment to gender equality. It has been written to help staff and volunteers ensure that our work improves the lives of both women and men and promotes gender equality.

Principles

- Throughout the organisation, we will base our work on a common understanding that gender equality is key to overcoming poverty and suffering.

- We will work with both women and men to address the specific ideas and beliefs that create and reinforce gender related poverty.

- Women and girls will be empowered through all aspects of our programme and ways of working, and we will often prioritise work which specifically raises the status of women.

- Our own internal practices, and ways of working, will reflect our commitment to gender equality.

Strategies for achieving gender equality

- A thorough understanding of the different concerns, experiences, capacities and needs of women and men, will shape the way we analyse, plan, implement and evaluate all our work.

- We will address the policies, practices, ideas and beliefs that perpetuate gender inequality and prevent women and girls (and sometimes men and boys) from enjoying a decent livelihood, participation in public life, protection and basic services.

---

1 Adapted from Marsha Freeman, Oxfam GB Gender Review, September 2001

- We will seek to ensure the full participation and empowerment of women in all areas of our work, and will promote women's rights as human rights, particularly in the areas of abuse and violence.

- We will work with both men and women, together and separately, to have a more lasting impact on beliefs and behaviour. We will ensure that any work we do with men and men's groups supports the promotion of gender equality.

- Partnerships and alliances will be assessed on the basis of their commitment to gender equality.

- Our campaign, advocacy and media messages, and the images we use to support these, will emphasise the importance of gender equality in overcoming poverty and suffering. Our communications will also highlight our own commitment to gender equality, and the essential role played by women in all aspects of development and humanitarian work.

- Managers will encourage groups and forums across the organisation to share learning and best practice on gender equality. Gender training will also be made available to staff and volunteers.

- In all our work we will demonstrate commitment to gender equality through setting appropriate team and individual objectives, and through allocating adequate staff and resources to enable us to fulfil the gender equality policy.

- Managers of all divisions will devise and report on measurable objectives and actions relating to the gender equality policy; and our management, finance and human resource systems will facilitate and contribute to our gender work.

- Gender awareness and understanding will be used as a criterion for recruitment and development of staff and volunteers.

- Within the organisation we will pursue family-friendly work practices that enable both men and women to participate fully in work and family life.

This gender policy is closely linked to Oxfam's Equal Opportunities and Diversity Policies.

Supplementary information (4)
Oxfam GB Child-Protection Policy

(Not a handout – for the facilitator only)

Date first approved   September 2004
Date for renewal   September 2006
Geographical scope   Worldwide

Policy Statement: Oxfam GB believes that all children under the age of 18 have the right to protection from abuse and exploitation, and recognises its responsibility to ensure that staff, volunteers, consultants and partners are clear about the standards of behaviour and practice that are required of them when in contact with children, at all times. Oxfam GB will develop measures and mechanisms to prevent abuse, protect staff and safeguard the reputation of the organisation.

Confidentiality: The policy statement will be made public. Other policy details are internal to staff and volunteers.

Purpose of Policy: The purpose of the policy is to set minimum standards by which all managers, staff and others carrying out work for Oxfam GB are expected to abide.

Policy Details: Abuse and exploitation can occur in many different forms. They can include neglect or bullying or be physical, sexual or emotional. Whilst abuse and exploitation of children can occur anywhere, it is accepted that as an international aid agency, our beneficiaries may be particularly vulnerable in this respect.

Code of Conduct: Oxfam GB's Code of Conduct outlines the standards expected of Oxfam GB staff. The Code of Conduct forms part of the terms and conditions of employment. A similar Code of Conduct has been produced, which relates specifically to volunteers, consultants and contractors and will form part of their 'contract' with Oxfam GB. Managers are responsible for explaining the Code of Conduct to their staff so that they understand what is expected of them. Guidelines are also available on 'Good practice when working with children'.

Reporting Procedures: Whilst different cultures may have different levels of tolerance, Oxfam GB will not tolerate what it considers to be abuse or exploitation in any form, which goes against the beliefs, values and aims of the organisation. It is the responsibility of all who represent Oxfam GB, in whatever capacity, to raise their concerns appropriately.

Any member of staff having concerns regarding possible issues of abuse or exploitation in projects managed or supported by Oxfam GB, or is aware that a member of staff is committing abuse, should raise these immediately through their line management, using the Disclosure of Malpractice Procedures. If it is not possible to do this with an immediate line manager, issues should be taken to the next level of management; see procedures for details. Complaints of this nature raised by non-staff members should use the formal complaints procedures. Any concerns raised will be treated with the utmost urgency, consideration and discretion.

Action taken against individuals who are believed to have abused or exploited a child/children may vary in each country context according to local cultures and legal frameworks. For members of staff, procedures within Oxfam GB's "Problems at Work" policy will be followed, and the matter may also be referred to the appropriate legal authority.

Recruitment Procedures: All recruiting managers are expected to follow Oxfam GB's recruitment and selection procedures to ensure that where a staff member will be working with children (those under the age of 18), either directly or indirectly, the necessary checks have been carried out to ensure that there is no known reason why they should not be employed to work with children, such as previous history of child abuse or exploitation. See Recruitment and Selection Guidelines.

This is particularly important for recruitment to posts in humanitarian situations, where it is essential to get staff to an area as quickly as possible. Specifically,

- Oxfam GB's online recruitment system or a standard application form must be used in all cases. This will help to establish previous criminal convictions and will provide structured details of skills and experience.
- Evidence of specific professional and personal qualifications must be checked.
- Rigorous checking of experience and gaps in employment history should be carried out.

Specific questions should be used during the interview to:

- test levels of awareness of the problems of child abuse and the risks to children relevant to the position applied for,
- check out the individual's commitment to the principles and values of Oxfam GB,
- reinforce positive messages regarding the protection of children from abuse, and
- gather a sense of the individual's personal and professional values and practices in this respect.

Check legitimate registers (such as police records) in all cases where the individual is likely to come into unsupervised contact with vulnerable groups.

References. Two references must be taken out before the appointment of any member of staff. Where the post involves working with or having significant contact with children, a specific question should be asked about their suitability to work with children.

There may be a temptation to omit stages of the recruitment procedures, such as reference checks. This is a risk that Oxfam GB is not prepared to take. References <u>must</u> be taken prior to staff starting work.

Guidelines: Advice on working with children can be found in *The Oxfam Handbook of Development and Relief* (Volume 1, page 269). Knowing what to do when there is evidence of, or appears to be, a situation of abuse in a local organisation can be very difficult. Reporting to authorities may not be viable, and withdrawing any funding or networking relationship may be the only solution. Possible options should be discussed with line managers.

Other relevant documents
Code of Conduct (Staff)
Code of Conduct (Non-Staff)
Dealing with Problems at Work
Disclosure of Malpractice (Policy and Guidelines)
Recruitment and Selection Guidelines
Young People and Children Working with Oxfam GB
External Complaints Procedure
Management Guidelines – Good Practice when Working with Children

Supplementary information (5)
Good practice when working with children
(Not a handout – intended for the facilitator only)

When in contact with children under the age of 18:

Always:

- Be aware of situations which may present risks, and manage these.

- Plan and organise the work and the workplace so as to minimise risks.

- Be visible to others when working with children whenever possible.

- Be open. Create and maintain a non-defensive attitude and an open culture in which to discuss any issues or concerns.

- Foster a culture of mutual accountability so that any potentially abusive behaviour can be challenged.

- Develop a culture where the children can talk about their contacts with staff and others openly.

- Respect each child's boundaries and help them to develop their own sense of their rights, as well as helping them to know what they can do if they feel there is a problem.

In general, it is inappropriate to:

- Spend excessive time alone with children away from others.

- Take children to your own home, especially where they will be alone with you.

Never:

- Hit or otherwise physically assault or physically abuse children.

- Develop physical/sexual relationships with children.

- Develop relationships with children which could in any way be deemed as exploitative or abusive.

- Act in ways that may be abusive or may place a child at risk of abuse.

- Use language, make suggestions or offer advice which is inappropriate, offensive or abusive.

- Behave physically in a manner that is inappropriate or sexually provocative.

- Have a child/children with whom you are working to stay overnight at your home, unsupervised.

- Sleep in the same room or bed as a child with whom you are working.

- Do things of a personal nature for children which they can do for themselves.

- Condone, or participate in, behaviour of children that is illegal, unsafe or abusive.

- Act in ways intended to shame, humiliate, belittle or degrade.

- Discriminate against, show different treatment to, or favour particular children to the exclusion of others.

Many thanks to Tearfund for allowing us to reproduce and use their 'Guidelines for Good Practice'.

Preventing Sexual Exploitation and Abuse

A Training Course for Managers

One day or half a day, as appropriate

Written by Yoma Winder

(Oxfam GB Humanitarian Programme Adviser)

with help, support, and contributions from many staff of Oxfam GB around the world

Preventing Sexual Exploitation and Abuse
A Training Course for Managers

Contents

Facilitator's notes

Handouts

Flipcharts 188

Supplementary information

PowerPoint slides 216

Introduction

Information for managers

Module length

One day or half a day, depending on the time available. A full day is preferable, for both facilitator and learners.

Facilitation skills

- This module requires presentation skills and the management of facilitated discussion and small-group activities.

- The level of facilitation skills required for this course will be determined by the degree of behavioural change that the workshop is required to deliver.

- Ideally the facilitator should have a helper who can deal with the large number of flipcharts on which this course is based. The helper might also lead some of the sessions, so that participants get to see a different face.

- Participants will raise questions about the Oxfam Code of Conduct and Sexual Conduct. The facilitator needs to be able to answer and debate these, and defend and promote Oxfam's positions, or to have someone else in the room who can act as an expert resource person.

- Ideally the facilitator should have had some degree of exposure to Oxfam's Code of Conduct and should have experience of making management decisions on staff conduct.

- Local managers are responsible for ensuring that this workshop is delivered by a facilitator who has sufficient experience and competence.

Learners

This module is intended for the following learners:

- All categories of staff, ranging from those in senior regional positions to those at local project-officer level.*

- All those who manage staff or programmes, or advise others how to do so.

- Those who will be responsible for explaining Oxfam's position and its implementation to Oxfam GB partners.

*A separate module is available in this pack to provide training for drivers, guards, programme support staff, field workers, workers in camp situations, etc.

Prerequisites for learners

This course is intended for all staff from middle to senior grades. It is especially relevant to those who manage or who will be managing staff in emergency-relief situations; therefore these staff should be given priority. Before the course begins, participants should be asked to write a half-page account of an incident that they have experienced or have witnessed which touches upon sexual exploitation or abuse in some way. Participants should be sent the instructions and guidelines, supplied here as 'Supplementary 1', at least ten days before the date of the course.

Group size

This course could be run for groups of 6 to 36 people, but ideally the group should number between 12 and 20.

Information for facilitators

Room

This module requires space for the whole group to work together in one room, seated in such a way that they can all see one another. It also requires sufficient space for the group to divide into smaller groups.

Equipment needed

- 2 flipchart stands, plenty of flipchart paper, and pens (black or dark blue to ensure visibility).
- Laptop and data projector for best results, **or**
- Overhead projector and acetates
- Post-it notes
- Blu-Tack

Preparation of material

- Photocopy the four handouts (1 – 4).
- Write up pre-prepared flipcharts (1 – 11). Use only black or blue pens, so that writing will be visible to all.
- Decide whether you prefer to use a data projector or an overhead projector. If you are going to use an overhead projector, you will need to copy on to acetate sheets the pages of the two PowerPoint presentations PPT1 (pages 216–224) and PPT2 (pages 225–233).
- Print the supplementary material (2 – 4) that you will need to present and facilitate the course. It is important to remember that this supplementary material is provided for you, not for the participants. It is not, under any circumstances, to be handed to participants.
- The participants need to prepare, in advance, a written description of an incident of sexual exploitation or abuse that they have experienced or witnessed (either within a working environment or outside it). Cut and paste the explanatory text contained in Supplementary Information (1) and send it to the applicants by email, fax, or post, at least 10 days before the day of the course.
- Identify and instruct two volunteers for the story-telling exercise (if you are doing the full-day session).

Preparation of the facilitator

The facilitator needs to read and study all the material before the day of the course.

- It is essential for the facilitator to be thoroughly familiar with the supplementary information (2 – 4) before the course begins. These **should not be given to the participants**. Oxfam staff: if you want to read more about the subject and feel fully prepared to answer as many questions as possible, read the extra optional information on the Intranet:
- Anti-Harrassment Policy http://homepage.oxfam.org.uk/chr/polproc/7/harass.htm
- Behaviour at Work http://homepage.oxfam.org.uk/chr/polproc/10/behaviouratworkhomepage.htm
- Dealing with Problems at Work http://homepage.oxfam.org.uk/chr/polproc/7/problemsatwork.htm

In addition, sample flipcharts are included in the pack. They are numbered 1 – 11 and are intended to give an idea of how the flipcharts should look.

Linked learning

- Oxfam staff should feel free to ask their regional focal points, Human Resources team, or line manager for support before or after running the sessions.
- It is the responsibility of every individual to promote and uphold the principles that will reduce the likelihood of sexual exploitation and abuse being committed by NGO staff. Please ensure that you take every opportunity to discuss this subject with your colleagues.

Translations

This module is currently available in English, Spanish, French, and Portuguese. If it would help learners, please feel free to translate all or part of it into additional languages – but please send a copy to Oxfam Publishing, Oxfam House, at the address given at the front of this pack.

Support and feedback

- Please send questions, ideas, and feedback to learninternational@oxfam.org.uk

Workshop objectives

Participants will:

Know ...

- The principles that underpin Oxfam GB's Code of Conduct and the Guidelines for Sexual Conduct

Feel ...

- Confident to make judgements and decisions on the sensitive and difficult subject of sexual exploitation and abuse.

Do ...

- Study cases of sexual exploitation and abuse in order to see where decisions need to be taken and, in some cases, how they could have been improved.

- Reflect on personal cases, discuss and analyse them to identify important issues, decisions, and judgements, and write these up for further use.

Participants will have an increased knowledge of and ability to comply with Oxfam's Internal Staff Code of Conduct. Managers will feel more confident to use the Code, and all staff participating will understand the responsibilities that it implies and demands.

Timetable

Full-day session		
Start	Finish	Session
00.00	00.15	1. Introductions
00.15	00.30	2. Story telling
00.30	00.50	3. Quiz
00.50	01.30	4. Presentation
01.30	01.45	BREAK
01.45	02.25	5. Exercise – OGB's Code of Conduct
02.25	02.55	6. Exercise – OGB's Sexual Conduct Guidelines
02.55	03.25	7. Brainstorm: vulnerable beneficiaries
03.25	04.25	LUNCH
04.25	04.40	8. Checking on the objectives of the course
04.40	05.40	9. Case studies
05.40	05.55	10. Story telling in groups
05.55	06.10	Break
06.10	07.15	11. Group work on chosen stories
07.15	07.45	12. Evaluation
07.45	08.00	13. Review and summary

Half-day session		
Start	Finish	Session
00.00	00.15	1. Introductions
00.15	00.45	2. Quiz
00.45	01.25	3. Presentation
01.25	02.05	4. Exercise – OGB's Code of Conduct
02.05	02.35	5. Exercise – OGB's Sexual Conduct Guidelines
02.35	02.50	BREAK
02.50	03.50	6. Case studies
03.50	04.00	7. Evaluation
N.B. If time permits, the Facilitator may choose to include sessions 10 and 11 from the full-day timetable.		

The timings for this event are shown as starting from 00.00.
The precise times should be adjusted to fit in with the group's
normal working hours.

Note to the facilitator

The subjects of sexual conduct, exploitation, and abuse nearly always raise more questions than they answer. Although the debates that occur are always stimulating, you should be aware that people feel strong emotions when their beliefs and personal values are challenged. Make sure that you read all the supplementary documentation (2 – 4) before delivering the session, and be sure that you can defend the positions taken in it.

Please remember, and emphasise to participants, that we run these workshops because we know that many beneficiaries are forced into sexual relations with humanitarian workers in order to get food, goods, or essential services for themselves and their families. Oxfam GB finds this intolerable and will do everything that it can to prevent it happening. Those found sexually exploiting or abusing beneficiaries will (subject to due process) be dismissed for gross misconduct.

The discussions during the day will raise many important issues, but it is important to move the course along and delay questions until the relevant session, when they might be covered anyway.

- Pay careful attention to the timings of the course and be prepared to chair the event firmly. Remember that not every question can be asked or answered within the course of one day.

- Put a page of flipchart paper on the wall to 'park' questions that arise. This is a clear way of acknowledging a question without having to answer it at that time – but if you have not answered all of the questions by the end of the course, you should clearly identify the means by which you will answer them (for example, by consulting an appropriate colleague and then sending the answer by email to all of the participants).

- In order to maintain the pace and energy of the course, you need to be very clear about timings and instructions. If you give 10 minutes for groups to do an exercise, after 5 minutes you should announce that 5 minutes remain; after 9 minutes, announce that one minute remains – and then finish after one more minute. You will find that groups often produce better results if they are under a reasonable degree of pressure.

Session 1   Introductions

TOTAL TIME: 15 minutes

Purpose: By the end of this session, participants will know the aim of this workshop and will know who is in the room. In addition they will begin to know what the organisation expects of them in terms of their sexual conduct. (The reasons will be discussed in later sessions.)

Timing	What YOU do	What the LEARNERS do	Resources
00.00	• Introduce yourself. • Ask the participants to introduce themselves briefly by telling the group their name, their job title, and the country or project area in which they work.	• Ask questions if they need clarification. • Introduce themselves, but very briefly.	
00.05	• Introduce the course objectives by showing flipcharts F1a and F1b. Attach them to the wall so they can be seen throughout the session. Read them aloud to participants and ask if they have any questions. • Give flipchart F2 to a participant and ask him or her to read it aloud to the group. Tell the group to think about it but not to comment at this stage – unless they need any explanation. Ask the participant to put flipchart F2 on the wall somewhere visible. Don't spend much time on this. There will be plenty of time for discussion during the day. • Give flipchart F3 to a different participant and ask him or her to read it aloud. Ask the group for their thoughts on these responsibilities. Ask them to recall occasions when they took the initiative to ensure an environment that reduced the risk of sexual exploitation or abuse of beneficiaries. Try to get two or three examples. • Read through flipchart F4 aloud. • Introduce the idea of a 'parking' flipchart (F5), where you will write up questions that cannot be answered immediately. It is your responsibility to ensure that the questions on flipchart (F5) are directed, after the event, to those who can answer them.	• Read the objectives and compare them with their own understanding and expectation of the course. • Read flipcharts F2 and F3 and think about their relevance to their own work. • Try to think of examples of when they have actively promoted behaviour or activities that have reduced the risk of exploitation or abuse of beneficiaries. • Listen to the examples given, and try to relate them to their own working lives – have they seen, done or thought about anything similar? Could they replicate the example given?	• Flipchart s F1a and F1b (Objectives) • Flipchart F2 (Rules) • Flipchart F3 (Responsibilities) • Flipchart F4 (Agenda) • Flipchart F5 (for parking questions)
00.15			

Session 2　　Storytelling

TOTAL TIME:
15 minutes

Purpose: Participants will share at least 3 short stories of sexual exploitation and abuse that they have seen or heard about, either at work or outside work. It is important that people start talking about this sensitive subject as soon as possible.

Timing	What YOU do	What the LEARNERS do	Resources
00.15	• Using flipchart F6, remind them about the need to respect confidential information. • Emphasise the fact that breaches of confidentiality will be considered a disciplinary offence. • Tell a short story of sexual abuse or exploitation that you have witnessed or experienced. If you cannot provide one, then use one from the 'prepared stories' (Supplementary Information 2). • Before the course started, you will have briefed two or more participants to 'volunteer' to share with the group a short story about the exploitation or abuse of beneficiaries in a programme of humanitarian relief. Choose people who will speak briefly. You should verify in advance that their stories are short, informative, and anonymous. • Find these two 'volunteers' now and ask them to tell their stories to the group.	• Listen to stories told by other participants. Relate the stories to their own lives or experiences. Consider how the stories relate to the example that they themselves have prepared.	• Flipchart F6 (Confident-iality)
00.30	• It is possible that there may be time for only two stories. You should keep an eye on the time and judge for yourself how many to include in this session.		

Session 3   Quiz

TOTAL TIME: 20 minutes

Purpose: another warm-up for the later sessions. A brief introduction to some of the ideas and terminology that will be used during the day.

Timing	What YOU do	What the LEARNERS do	Resources
00.30	• Choose either a data processor or overhead projector and the appropriate information format for presenting.	• Answer the questions as and when they can.	• Laptop and data projector
	• Tell the participants that they are about to do a light-hearted quiz (PPT1). They will not know all the answers, but they should shout out the answers that they think they do know.	• Make it clear if they don't understand the answers, or if they need more detail.	• PPT1 slide show (quiz) or OHP and slides
	• Go quite fast through the quiz: you read the questions out loud, but make the participants produce the answers.		
	• The aim of the quiz is for you to gain some idea of how much participants know about the subject and some related issues. It does not matter if the answers are right or wrong; the purpose of the quiz is to encourage active participation.		
	• Encourage all the participants to respond, not just the loud and confident ones. At this stage you should encourage everyone to feel relaxed, and to think and contribute as much as possible.		
	Notes on the quiz:		
	• Using the PowerPoint presentation is easiest, because it gives participants time to shout out their answers.		
	• If you are using slides and an OHP, you can put each transparency on the OHP and cover up the answer until the group have given some answers.		
	• Before the day begins, read through the quiz enough times to be able to anticipate the answers. Read the policies and guidelines (Handouts 1 and 2).		
	• The quiz mentions 'gross misconduct'. Here is a definition: *gross misconduct is an act that is very likely to lead to summary dismissal with loss of most employment benefits.*		
00.50			

Session 4   Presentation   (4 pages)

TOTAL TIME: 40 minutes

Purpose: To give a brief overview of the nature and extent of the problem of abuse, and the work that Oxfam GB and others have done so far to address it. To show why and how Oxfam GB has initiated four major pieces of work to combat sexual abuse, and to demonstrate how this training course fits into the overall scheme of work that is to be done.

Timing	What YOU do	What the LEARNERS do	Resources
00.50	• Choose either a data projector or an overhead projector and the appropriate format for presenting. • Run the presentation (PPT2). • **Slide 1:** Read the title slide and draw learners' attention to the objectives of the training day. • **Slide 2:** Ask if they know anything about the scandal of sexual abuse committed by humanitarian workers in refugee camps in the Mano River region (Guinea, Liberia, and Sierra Leone) in 2001//02. If so, invite them to share what they know. • In those countries it was found, almost by accident, that abuses of refugees by humanitarian workers were taking place on a very large scale. Typically, sexual favours were being demanded of (and accepted from) beneficiaries in return for goods or services that were controlled by the humanitarian workers. More than 40 NGOs, both national and international, were implicated by name. Oxfam was not named, but this did not mean that some of our staff were not guilty of committing similar abuses. The scandal prompted all agencies to take the problem seriously, and the aid community began work to prevent it happening again.	• Listen to the presentation and ask questions if they need anything clarified. Questions that are impossible to answer should be written on the 'parking' flipchart. • If they know anything about the problems mentioned in the slide, they should share that information.	• Laptop and data projector or OHP and slides • PPT2 • Flipchart F5 (for parking questions)

- In 2001 the media obtained reliable information that UNHCR staff and project partners were committing abuses against Bhutanese women and children in refugee camps in Nepal. The abuses included trafficking of women and organising and profiting from their prostitution. Oxfam and UNHCR (and possibly many others) had known about this for some time. When the scandal became public, UNHCR admitted some degree of liability. Good work was done to prevent a recurrence of the abuses.

- In 2003 the UN system began to investigate allegations of abuse and exploitation by its peace-keeping force (MONUC) in Democratic Republic of Congo. There was clear evidence of widespread and severe abuse. Currently investigations into the behaviour of more than 130 UN personnel (both military and civilian) are pending.

- Emphasise the point that these abuses really do happen in the aid profession. There is plenty of convincing evidence to prove it. Oxfam has dismissed many staff on these grounds, but many more cases have not been dealt with, because managers were unaware, unwilling, or unable to deal with them. We do not expect managers who have taken part in this training course to avoid these issues in the future.

- **Slides 3 and 4:** These slides should help learners to understand why and how abuse can happen. Uneven balances of power probably always exist between agency workers and beneficiaries. But in humanitarian situations the differential is extreme. Most beneficiaries (at least in the early stages of an emergency) are entirely dependent on agency workers for their very survival and that of their families. We have everything, and they have nothing. It is easy for humanitarian workers to exploit this difference in power, and it is usual for beneficiaries to want or need them to do so, in order to obtain what they need for themselves and their families. This type of transaction gradually becomes the norm, and most of those involved fail to appreciate the nature or seriousness of the problem.

- Participants should think about themselves and their jobs, and the realities of beneficiaries' lives, to appreciate how easy it is for abuse and exploitation to occur.

- Ask questions if they do not understand.

- Ensure that questions that can't be answered now are written on Flipchart F5.

- **Slide 5:** Show the title of this slide and ask the group to suggest why this sort of behaviour is problematic, and what the consequences of it might be for a project or programme or country team. It is important to emphasise the indirect impact on other agencies in the sector: if one agency is known to have committed abuses, we will all be blamed, and suspicion will lie upon us all.

  - Think about what it would mean to their organisation if a member of staff was behaving badly towards beneficiaries, and the beneficiary community and general public became aware of it.

- **Slides 6 and 7:** Ensure that participants understand that 'in the line' probably involves them, because they are managers! Return to Flipchart F3 ('roles and responsibilities') at this point if participants are not convinced. It is very important that they realise that this training course is all about THEM – because most managers have felt unwilling or unable to deal with such issues in the past.

  - Participants should think about what this means for them personally. How easy or difficult will it be to deal with allegations of abuse? Have they ever dealt with things like this before? What happened then? How would they like to be able to react in a similar situation after this training session?

- Check that learners understand the concepts of 'focal point' and 'champion'. In Oxfam terms, they denote members of staff within each region or programme where abuse is considered likely to take place who, in addition to their normal jobs, are responsible for leading and supporting work to improve the attitudes and behaviour of staff.

  - Think about the use of focal points (or other initiatives). What could they personally do to support the work of focal points?

- All staff and managers must understand that they share responsibility for preventing the abuse and exploitation of vulnerable beneficiaries. As the facilitator, you should emphasise this point throughout the training. This scandal is not confined to other people in other organisations: it can occur in any agency, anywhere – and often does.

- **Slide 8:** This is the support that is available to Oxfam staff and managers. Facilitators on non-Oxfam courses might want to research this matter in advance of the session. Find out what is available and appropriate for the participants whom you are training. Or ensure that questions about this matter are put on the parking flipchart (F5) and answered, quickly, after the session.

  - Participants might be able to suggest what would be useful to them in terms of support. Suggestions should be written on flipchart F5.

Slide 9: These are the issues that concern Oxfam GB. They will not be appropriate for all agencies. However, they are fairly common dilemmas, so it may be useful to discuss them.

- Organisations need to know what their donors expect from them in terms of staff behaviour and attitudes. And they need to align their Code of Conduct and training accordingly. Oxfam GB has done this to a certain extent and will do more work on it in the near future. In particular we will continue to consider our policy on the matter of paying for sex with professional sex workers.

  - Think about these issues and what they would mean in practice. Share relevant experience or suggestions with the group.

- In general, agencies like Oxfam expect partner organisations to share their values and beliefs. But it might not be appropriate to expect them to adhere to exactly the same Code of Conduct. A reasonable compromise can often be reached by including a statement about behaviour in the contract or Memorandum of Understanding that is signed when a partnership is established.

- Inductions, training, and support must be adapted to suit the needs of individual organisations. Oxfam will continue to seek advice on how to improve its processes in order to respond to the risk of abuse and exploitation. Participants' feedback on this training session will be sought in the evaluation session(s) at the end of the day.

- Oxfam GB has found that the best way of communicating its concerns about abuse to its overseas offices, and ensuring their commitment to tackle it, is by nominating, training, and supporting Focal Points. Key staff, who have experience and wisdom, have been asked to provide information, advice, and support to any staff who think they have a problem or who have seen behaviour that troubles them. Focal Points are not 'in the line' and are not expected to make decisions or take action: their remit is to give advice and support to those in management positions.

  - Think about whether they would like to become focal points within their programme or country or region. If so, they should inform the facilitator.

01.30

01.30 – 01.45	BREAK
	Encourage the group to move from their chairs and take some refreshments. When we are learning, it is important to have time to reflect. Ask the group not to use the break as an opportunity to make telephone calls or return to their desks.

Those who have not yet prepared a story to tell **must** now do so. Encourage participants to talk to each other to help them to think of a good example. |

Session 5   Exercise 1: Oxfam GB's Code of Conduct

TOTAL TIME: 40 minutes

Purpose: to encourage participants to look closely at the Code and identify absolute instructions and then issues that are less clearly defined. To identify what the Code really does and does not permit Oxfam GB staff to do.

Timing	What YOU do	What the LEARNERS do	Resources
01.45	• Uncover flipchart F7 and read the instructions aloud. • Repeat the instruction to read only the 'Standards' section of Handout 1 – the rest can be read later. • Ask participants to form pairs and list three activities that the Code definitely forbids, and three issues which they feel are less clearly defined. • Set a time limit of 30 minutes. • Check with participants that they understand what to do. • Give each learner a copy of the Code of Conduct (Handout 1). • Walk round, encouraging discussion and answering queries. • If pairs finish early, encourage them to discuss their findings with others. • Give 10-minute and 5-minute warnings before the end of discussion time.	• Divide into pairs. • Make sure they understand the instructions. • Read pages 2 and 3 of the Code of Conduct together. Leave the rest until later. • Pick out three areas/activities that they think the Code is clear about, and three areas/activities on which they need more clarity.	• Handout 1: one copy for each participant • Flipchart F7, with the task explained • Flipchart for answers
02.15	• Bring the group back together. • Ask each pair in turn to report **one** example of a clear instruction or **one** example of an unclear instruction. • Write these up on separate flipchart sheets. • Tell participants that the issues identified as 'unclear' will be reported to the advisers who are working to refine the Code. • Oxfam facilitators: keep the flipchart for feeding back to your regional focal point!	• Give one example of a clear or unclear aspect of the Code.	• Flipchart for feedback
02.25			

Session 6   Exercise 2: Oxfam GB's guidelines on sexual conduct

TOTAL TIME:
30 minutes

Purpose: to help participants to understand the underlying principles upon which rules for the sexual conduct of Oxfam GB staff are based. To help them to realise the responsibility that Oxfam places on them to create and maintain conditions in which adherence to the Code can be ensured.

Timing	What YOU do	What the LEARNERS do	Resources
02.25	• Ask participants to form groups of 5 or 6. • Read out the instructions for the exercise from flipchart F8. • Introduce flipcharts 8a, 8b, 8c, 8d, and 8e. Ask five participants to stick them up in separate parts of the room and read them aloud, one after the other. ■ Give out Handout 2: Guidelines for Sexual Conduct. Tell participants that they have 10 minutes to read and discuss it. Explain that once they have read the document they will be asked, as a group, to respond to each of the questions in turn. It does not matter which question they start with, but they must have a response or a comment to make on each question. ■ This exercise requires the groups to get up and move round the room, writing comments and questions on each flipchart. • The first two or three answers on any one flipchart might take some time (3 or 4 minutes). After this you should speed up the exercise, giving groups two minutes in front of each flipchart.	• Get into small groups. • Stick up flipcharts as requested, read aloud if asked. ■ Read Handout 2 and discuss in groups the answers to the questions posed, or their comments on the questions. ■ Think hard about the implications of these guidelines for themselves and for their team. Think about the need to regulate/change behaviour or thinking in any way. ■ Get up and move around the room, writing answers or comments on the flipcharts as requested.	■ Handout 2: one copy for each participant ■ Flipchart F8 with instructions for the exercise ■ 5 flipcharts (F8a, b, c, d, e) with questions already written on them
02.45	• Ask one participant to read aloud from one flipchart the original questions and the group's written responses. Ask learners what they think of the comments and answers. Is everybody in agreement? Repeat this for each of the flipcharts. • With Oxfam staff, reassure them that unresolved or difficult issues will be referred back to the 'sexploitation' focal point or the relevant adviser in the Humanitarian Department • Oxfam facilitators: keep the flipchart for feeding back to your regional focal point!	• Think about what others have written. • Think about the implications for their own work and the work of their teams. • Raise issues that they don't understand or agree with.	
02.55			

TOTAL TIME: 30 minutes

Session 7   Brainstorm: vulnerable beneficiaries

Purpose: to stimulate participants to think about why beneficiaries in their region/country/project area might be particularly vulnerable to sexual exploitation and abuse.

Timing	What YOU do	What the LEARNERS do	Resources
02.55	<ul><li>Ask participants to form groups of 5 or 6.</li><li>Uncover flipchart F9, which describes the task.</li><li>Give out one piece of flipchart paper per group. Ask them to brainstorm the particular features of their region/country/ project area that would make beneficiaries vulnerable to sexual abuse or exploitation.</li><li>Offer some suggestions of your own, e.g.<ul><li>women have no or little status in law</li><li>chronic conflict has erased people's sense of what is normal or right</li><li>the supply chain of goods for beneficiaries is inadequate</li><li>there is a high level of domestic violence.</li></ul></li><li>Give a reminder 5 minutes and 1 minute from the end of the allotted time.</li></ul>	<ul><li>Form small groups.</li><li>Write up reasons why beneficiaries in their area might be vulnerable to sexual abuse, bearing in mind the specific contexts in which they work and in which the beneficiaries live.</li></ul>	• Flipchart F9
03.15	<ul><li>From one participant at a time, gather suggested reasons why women and children might be particularly vulnerable at this time or in this particular context. Ask each person for one suggestion and then move on to the next person, to ensure that all members of the group have a chance to speak and share their ideas.</li><li>Invite comments from other participants.</li><li>Pin the flipchart paper to the wall for later use.</li><li>Oxfam facilitators: keep the flipcharts for feeding back to your regional exploitation focal point!</li></ul>	<ul><li>Volunteer answers, comment on the answers of others.</li></ul>	
03.25			

03.25 – 04.25   LUNCH BREAK
It is important to have time to reflect on what has been learned, so ask the group not to use the break as an opportunity to make telephone calls or return to their desks.

TOTAL TIME:
15 minutes

Session 8   Checking the objectives of the course

Purpose: to reassure participants that they are on the way to meeting the objectives of the day.

Timing	What YOU do	What the LEARNERS do	Resources
04.25	• Ask participants to read the objectives on flipchart F1a. • Ask them to tell their neighbours one thing that they learned during the morning session which accords with the objectives. • Ask participants to discuss with their neighbours if and how they will change their thinking or behaviour as a result of this acquired knowledge. • Ask 4 or 5 participants to share their learning experiences with the group. • Ask the participants what they feel they still need to learn from the next few sessions.	• Read flipchart F1a. • Think about what they have learned this morning and discuss it with a neighbour. Think about how this learning will change the way they think or act. • Share a learning point with the group if asked. • Think about what still needs to be learned in order to achieve the objectives • Share this with the group if asked.	• Flipchart F1a (objectives)
04.40	• Reassure participants that in the afternoon sessions they will practise making decisions based on the knowledge gained this morning.		

Session 9   Case studies   (2 pages)

Purpose: to practise using new-found knowledge and confidence. To discuss cases where management decisions or judgements need to be made and what they should be.

TOTAL TIME:
60 minutes

Timing	What YOU do	What the LEARNERS do	Resources
04.40	• Ask participants to form groups of 5 or 6. • Uncover flipchart F10, showing the instructions for this exercise. • Tell learners to follow the instructions for each case study and write their answers on flipchart paper for sharing and discussing later. • Give one copy of Handout 3 to each participant. • Assign at least two case studies per group, in such a way that every case study is covered by at least one group, if possible. • Ensure that you have read, several times, the 'answers' to the case studies (Supplementary Information 3). Note that it is not always possible to give a completely definitive answer to the questions posed. Your job as facilitator is to encourage open discussion in which every member of the group participates. At the end of each discussion, you may choose to add a correction, *but it is not your role to give 'the answer'.* Note that S3 is not intended as a handout – it is provided to aid your own understanding as a facilitator. • It is very difficult to decide on appropriate sanctions in many of these cases. Rather than spending much time on this task, try to concentrate on what the managers would need to do to resolve the problem in its early stages and ensure that it does not recur. Obviously the sanctions play a part in this, but only a small part. • Circulate, intervening and prompting when necessary, and trying to ensure that everyone has a chance to speak, and that the discussions do not go too far off track.	• Concentrate on the case studies that they have been allocated, and follow the instructions for each case study carefully. • Write down their responses in order to share them with the rest of the group later.	• Flipchart F10, (instructions for the exercise) • Handout 3: one copy for each participant • Flipchart paper for each group of participants • Supplementary Information 3: Case Study 'answers'

Timing	What YOU do	What the LEARNERS do	Resources
	• Remind people that they have 10 minutes left, then 5, and then one.		
05.20	• Ask the groups to report back on their discussions, starting with case study number 1. • If more than one group has considered a particular case study, choose one group to present their responses and ensure that the other group(s) who have spent time on it get a chance to comment fully. • There will be plenty of discussion during the feedback session. Allow this to happen, but try to ensure that the debate covers all the items on the 'answer' sheet, and that the contributions to the debate are relevant to the central theme. • Make sure that one version of a generally 'correct' answer is clearly written up on a flipchart and displayed prominently on the wall.	• Report their own responses, and discuss the answers/comments of other groups.	• Flipchart paper for feedback
05.40			

Session 10   Story telling in groups

TOTAL TIME:
15 minutes

Purpose: for each small group to choose one real-life story, to serve as the basis for the following session.

Timing	What YOU do	What the LEARNERS do	Resources
05.40	• Ask the participants to form new groups of 5 or 6, working with people different from those with whom they worked in the previous session. • Tell groups that they have only 15 minutes to decide on the best story from the examples brought by the participants. The group will work on this story at greater length after the break. • In addition, remind all participants that, as stated in the preparatory memo (Supplementary Information 1) sent before the course began, confidentiality is absolutely essential. There will be no naming of people or places, so that confidentiality is ensured. Failure to respect this rule will be a disciplinary offence.	• Very briefly, tell their stories and choose the most appropriate.	
05.55			

05.55 – 06.10 BREAK
It is important while training to have time to reflect, so ask the group not to use the break as an opportunity to make telephone calls or return to their desks.

Session 11   Group work on chosen stories

TOTAL TIME: 65 minutes

Purpose: to practise new knowledge and decision-making skills in real-life case studies. To increase the stock of case studies by collecting all the stories brought to the workshop.

Timing	What YOU do	What the LEARNERS do	Resources

06.10	• Ask participants to return to their small groups.
	
	 • Ask each group to write up the example that they chose before the break. They should indicate where management decisions need to be made; the issues that managers must consider; and then the decisions that they as a group would have made as managers.
	
	 • With Oxfam staff, tell them that they will be asked to present this 'worked example' to the group as a whole, and to submit it to you, to help Oxfam to build up a 'bank' of good, real-life examples to use on further training courses.
	
	 • Remind all participants that confidentiality is absolutely essential. There will be no naming of people or places, in order to ensure confidentiality. Failure to respect this rule is a disciplinary offence. Refer them to flipchart F6.
	
	 • During the discussions, circulate among the groups in order to become familiar with all the examples. Guide the discussions as appropriate.
	
	 • Collect the stories that participants brought with them.
	
	 • Tell participants when 10 minutes remain, then 5 minutes, before the end of the session.
		• In small groups, work through their chosen examples, following instructions; e.g.
		  • What aspects of the story should concern managers?
		  • What should they do about this concern?
		  • What could be used as reference points, information points, or back-up to support the decision-making process?
		  • What other aspects of the context need to be brought into consideration?
		  • What decisions would you as managers have made if you had been in this situation?
		
		 • Write down their answers for submission to the facilitator and for presentation to the whole group.
		
		 • Give to the facilitator a copy of the case study / example that they each brought with them.
			• Flipchart F6
			
			 • Plenty of flipchart paper for participants to use

06.50	• Bring participants back together. • Instruct groups in turn to present and discuss their jointly chosen story. • Facilitate/mediate discussion as necessary, try to find 'right' answers.	• Listen to and comment on others' presentations. • Present one example per group. • Comment on others' examples.	
07.15	• Collect written copies of all the examples used.		

Session 12   Evaluation

TOTAL TIME: 25 Minutes

Purpose: to help participants to think of ways to improve their own performance, or that of others, in order to reduce the risk of beneficiaries being sexually exploited or abused. In Oxfam workshops: to generate ideas for information and action that the facilitator should send to the regional focal point.

Timing	What YOU do	What the LEARNERS do	Resources
07.15	• Put up flipchart F11. Give the participants 10 minutes to think about and answer the seven questions asked. • Give seven people the seven flipcharts (F11a, b, c, d, e, f, and g). Ask them to read the questions aloud, one after the other, and then stick them on the wall.	• Read the questions thoroughly. • Ask for clarification if necessary. • Mark their response to the questions asked. • Look at all the 'answers' and analyse how well the objectives have been achieved.	• Prepared flipcharts F11 and F11a, b, c, d, e, f, and g • Plenty of post-it notes.
0720	• Give each participant has a handful of post-it notes. • Start the exercise. • When it is completed, ask everybody to sit down again and comment on the results • Make your own comments, focusing on the following: • Issues which make people feel comfortable. • Issues which make people feel uncomfortable. • Any surprises.	• Think about the next step to help people to improve their performance where necessary. • Make suggestions to the group when asked.	
0735	▪ Ask participants to suggest ways of improving their performance.		
07.40			

Session 13   Review and summary

TOTAL TIME: 20 minutes

Purpose: to assess how the course worked for the participants, to find out if they have all the information that they need.

Timing	What YOU do	What the LEARNERS do	Resources
07.40	• Remind participants of the contents of Handouts 1, 2, and 3. Encourage them to go away and consider seriously the issue of sexual abuse and exploitation as it affects their work and the work of their teams. • Re-read Flipchart F3, on roles and responsibilities. • Ask them how they might do things differently in the future. • Reiterate that the main point of the whole day is to try to ensure that people are competent and confident to make decisions, using the Code of Conduct as a tool to regulate their own sexual conduct and that of Oxfam GB staff, and others. • Tell Oxfam staff that further advice can always be sought from their line manager, the regional focal point for sexual exploitation, and/or the humanitarian programme adviser in Oxfam House in Oxford.	• Make sure they each have a copy of all the handouts. • Make suggestions about future events – content, delivery, exercises, etc. • Ensure that they know who to turn to in future if they need help or support.	• Further copies of Handouts 1, 2, and 3 • Flipchart 3
07.55	• Give out copies of Handout 4 and ask the group to fill it in and hand it back to you before they leave. Tell the group that feedback is important, because it will help us to improve the training sessions in future.	• Fill in the feedback form.	• Handout 4 (feedback form)
08.00	• Collect the feedback forms. Oxfam facilitators: keep these for feedback to your regional focal point. • Thank the group for their time/energy etc. and assure them that answers to their questions on the 'parking' flipchart will be sent to them as soon as possible.		

Handout 1 (4 pages)
Oxfam GB Code of Conduct

INTRODUCTION

As an Oxfam GB staff member, you are required to abide by the organisation's policies and procedures, and the terms and conditions of your employment (as outlined in your employment contract), and to ensure your conduct is in keeping with the organisation's beliefs, values and aims.

The aim of this Code of Conduct is to give you guidance regarding the key issues that you need to be aware of as an Oxfam GB staff member, and the standards by which you may need to behave in certain circumstances. The Code applies to all Oxfam GB staff, regardless of location, and in accepting appointment you undertake to discharge your duties and to regulate your conduct in line with the requirements of this Code. The Code is designed for your guidance and protection, although a breach may result in disciplinary action (including dismissal in some instances) and, in some cases, may lead to criminal prosecution.

Whilst recognising that local laws and cultures differ considerably from one country to another, Oxfam GB is a British-based International NGO, and therefore the Code of Conduct is based on European and international legal standards, as well as being written to reflect the organisation's fundamental beliefs and values (as outlined below), to support its mission to work with others to overcome poverty and suffering, and its commitment to ensuring that staff members avoid using possible unequal power relationships for their own benefit.

OXFAM GB – MISSION, BELIEFS, AND VALUES

Oxfam GB's Purpose - To work with others to overcome poverty and suffering.

Oxfam GB's Beliefs -   The lives of all human beings are of equal value.
In a world rich in resources, poverty is an injustice which must be overcome.
Poverty makes people more vulnerable to conflict and natural calamity; much of this suffering can be prevented and must be relieved.
People's vulnerability to poverty and suffering is increased by unequal power relations based on, for example, gender, race, class, caste and disability; women, who make up the majority of the world's poor, are especially disadvantaged.
Working together we can build a just and safer world, in which people take control over their own lives and enjoy their basic rights.
To overcome poverty and suffering involves changing unjust policies and practices, nationally and internationally, as well as working closely with people in poverty.

Oxfam GB's Diversity - Oxfam GB recognises that our beliefs on equality are also relevant to
Policy   our ways of working. They relate to the way that we treat, work with and value those who are different from ourselves. We recognise that those who are different from ourselves should be treated with respect, have something positive to offer, and have an equal right to access resources and opportunities.

Oxfam GB's   Oxfam GB views all forms of harassment as incompatible with its
Anti-Harassment   aims and beliefs in the dignity of all people, and undermining to its
Policy   vision of equal opportunities. Consequently, Oxfam GB will not tolerate the harassment of staff, volunteers, contractors, partner organisations, beneficiaries or any others.

CODE OF CONDUCT – STANDARDS

As a staff member of Oxfam GB, I will:

1. **Be responsible for the use of information and resources to which I have access by reason of my employment with Oxfam GB.**
   - I will ensure that I use Oxfam GB information, funds, and resources entrusted to me in a responsible manner and account for all money and property, following the appropriate policy and procedural requirements. Resources and property include
         Oxfam GB vehicles
         Telephones, photocopiers, fax machines and stationery
         Other office equipment or equipment / resources belonging to Oxfam GB
         Computers, including the use of email, internet and intranet
         Oxfam GB accommodation (including Oxfam housing in international locations)

2. **Ensure the safety, health and welfare of all Oxfam GB staff members, volunteers and contractors.**
   - I will adhere to all legal and organisational health and safety requirements in force at the location of my work.
   - I will comply with any local security guidelines and be pro-active in informing management of any necessary changes to such guidelines.
   - I will behave in such a way as to avoid any unnecessary risk to the safety, health, and welfare of myself and others, including partner organisations and beneficiaries.

3. **Ensure that my personal and professional conduct is, and is seen to be, of the highest standards and in keeping with Oxfam GB's beliefs, values, and aims.**
   - I will treat all people fairly and with respect and dignity.
   - When working in an international context or travelling internationally on behalf of Oxfam GB, I will observe all local laws and be sensitive to local customs.
   - I will not work under the influence of alcohol or use, or be in possession of, illegal substances on Oxfam GB premises or accommodation.
   - I will seek to ensure that my sexual conduct does not bring Oxfam GB into any ill repute and does not impact on or undermine my ability to undertake the role for which I am employed.
   - I will not enter into commercial sex transactions with beneficiaries. For the purpose of this Code of Conduct, a transaction is classed as any exchange of money, goods, services or favours with any other person.

4. **Perform my duties and conduct my private life in a manner that avoids possible conflicts of interest with the work of Oxfam GB and my work as a staff member of the organisation.**
   - I will declare any financial, personal, family (or close intimate relationship) interest in matters of official business which may impact on the work of Oxfam GB – e.g. contract for goods/services, employment or promotion within Oxfam GB, partner organisations, civil authorities, beneficiary groups.
   - I will behave in a manner that does not undermine national or international perceptions of Oxfam GB's impartiality.
   - I will seek permission before agreeing to being nominated as a prospective candidate or another official role for any political party.
   - I will not accept any additional employment or consultancy work outside of Oxfam GB without prior permission from management.
   - I will not accept significant gifts or any remuneration from governments, beneficiaries, donors, suppliers and other persons which have been offered to me as a result of my employment with Oxfam GB.
   - I will not abuse my position as an Oxfam GB staff member by requesting any service or favour from others in return for assistance by Oxfam GB.

5. **Avoid involvement in any criminal activities, activities that contravene human rights, or those that compromise the work of Oxfam GB.**
   - I will contribute to combating all forms of illegal activities.
   - I will notify Oxfam GB of any unspent criminal convictions or charges prior to employment.
   - I will also notify the organisation if I face any criminal charges during my employment.
   - I will not engage in sexual behaviour with children under the age of 18, regardless of local custom.
   - I will not abuse or exploit children under the age of 18 in any way and will report any such behaviour of others to my line management.

6. **Refrain from any form of harassment, discrimination, physical or verbal abuse, intimidation or exploitation.**
   - I will fully abide by the requirements of Oxfam GB's equal opportunities, diversity, and anti-harassment policies.
   - I will never engage in any exploitative, abusive, or corrupt relationships.

I have read carefully and understand the Oxfam GB Code of Conduct and hereby agree to abide by its requirements and commit to upholding the standards of conduct required to support Oxfam GB's aims, values and beliefs.

Name ……………………………………………………………………………………………

Signature ………………………………………………………………………………………

Date ………………………………………………………………………………………………

APPLICATION OF THE CODE OF CONDUCT

The Code of Conduct is intended to serve as a guide for all Oxfam GB staff in making decisions in their professional lives and, at times, in their private lives. By following this Code of Conduct, it is intended that all staff will contribute to strengthening the professionalism and impact of the work of Oxfam GB.

The Code of Conduct forms part of the terms and conditions of employment of all staff. Further information and detail on specific aspects of this Code can also be found in Behaviour at Work in Oxfam GB's Policies and Procedures.

1. All staff will be given a copy of this Code and required to familiarise themselves with its requirements, by reading and discussing the Code with their manager or colleagues.
2. All staff will be required to confirm this by signing their agreement to the Code of Conduct and by keeping a copy. A further copy of the signed agreement will be kept on the staff member's personal file.
3. Further information on the provisions within the Code can be found in Oxfam GB's policies, procedures and guidelines. If needed, staff can also seek further clarification from their manager or a member of the Human Resources team.
4. For staff relocating to another country of work, guidance will also be given in relation to local specific customs and legal requirements, in order to inform the behaviour that they will be expected to adopt.
5. Further guidance and information will also be distributed to each office and work place and may also be found in related documents (e.g. Local Security Guidelines).
6. Managers have a responsibility to ensure that all staff, including newly recruited staff, are provided with a copy of the Code of Conduct, understand its provisions clearly, and sign their agreement to its terms.
7. Managers also have a particular responsibility to uphold the standards of conduct and to set an example.
8. In the recruitment and selection of staff, managers should seek to ensure that candidates selected support the beliefs and values of Oxfam GB and do not have a work history that contravenes the requirements of this Code.
9. Any staff member who has concerns about the behaviour of another staff member should raise these with the appropriate line manager. Any concerns will be treated with urgency, consideration and discretion.
10. Any breaches of the requirements of this Code of Conduct will be subject to investigation and possible disciplinary action in line with Oxfam GB's disciplinary procedure.

HANDOUT 2
Guidelines on Sexual Conduct
(from Oxfam GB's Code of Conduct)

Oxfam's Code of Conduct provides guidelines for the way Oxfam intends its staff to behave. The guidelines are necessarily broad, covering all aspects of behaviour, use of equipment, and guidance on relationships with others at many levels and in many situations.

The Code draws on and makes reference to many of Oxfam's policies: use of computers, harassment etc.; but there is no policy on sexual conduct or child protection. Below you will find a distillation of how Oxfam requires its staff to behave in this regard.

The underlying, non-negotiable principles that we expect to govern your behaviour and that of those around you are:

i. No exploitation or relationships that are exploitative as a result of your position within Oxfam.
ii. No actions that bring the organisation into disrepute.

Therefore

iii. No underage sex (because it is exploitative by nature).
iv. No sex with beneficiaries (because it is potentially exploitative by nature).

To clarify

v. When we say 'no sex', we mean no sexual contact whatsoever.
vi. There is equally little tolerance of either demanding *or accepting* sex or sexual contact in return for goods or services from you or Oxfam.

It is really important to stress that

vii. **It is your duty and responsibility to report, via the systems that exist, behaviour that you feel is not in accordance with the above edicts.**
viii. **It is also your responsibility to actively promote and maintain an atmosphere or environment in which staff feel that they can and will live up to the expectations clarified above.**

Handout 3 (3 pages)
Case Studies: Use of the Oxfam GB Code of Conduct

The following case studies are fictional, but each is based on elements of fact.

1   Use of Oxfam laptop to access pornographic websites

1a   First Scenario

A local staff member has admitted accessing pornographic websites via an Oxfam laptop.
The staff member is known to have received a full and correct induction, which included a good
briefing on the Code of Conduct and a detailed explanation and discussion of illegal/illicit use of
Oxfam's equipment.

1b   Second Scenario

A local staff member has admitted accessing pornographic websites via an Oxfam laptop. The
staff member has not received a briefing by either the line manager or Human Resources staff.

1c   Third Scenario

A local staff member has admitted accessing pornographic websites on an Oxfam computer.
His defence (which he doesn't really think he needs) is that it is culturally acceptable in his
country (and the country in which he is based) to do this, and he doesn't understand why Oxfam
finds fault with this. You cannot be sure that he has received a full and useful briefing on
Oxfam's Code of Conduct.

What would be your action/guidance in each of the above circumstances? Please indicate
where you think that KEY management decisions need to be made. Include follow-up actions
as appropriate.

2   Personal relationships

It comes to the attention of the Regional Programme Manager (you) and the Regional Director
that rumours are circulating regarding an expatriate Programme Coordinator in Country X. It is
claimed that the staff member, who is male, has been having a relationship with a local woman
who is rumoured to be a prostitute. Prostitution is illegal in Country X. Due to local custom and the
small and remote location of the town in which Oxfam is based, both the relationship and the
rumours are causing tension among local staff and arguably bringing the organisation into
disrepute. You know that the staff member has been fully and adequately briefed on Oxfam's
Code of Conduct both by you and the Human Resources team in the country.

Please think through the options given below, and decide which path you would take. Discuss the
various decisions that need to be taken, and the reasons for your choice.

Would you …
Decide that this behaviour is something that needs action in some way? *Why?*
Decide that this is something you can safely ignore and not do anything about it? *Why?*

Would you …
Phone the staff member in question and confront him with your thoughts? *Why?*
Find an opportunity to recall the staff member to the Regional Management Centre and have a
meeting with him? *Why?*
Find the earliest opportunity to visit the field office and try, without prior prejudice, to understand
the situation? *Why?*

Would you …
Make the process formal or informal at this stage? *Why?*

Would you …
Listen to staff member, take his point of view into account and find a way forward together? *Why?*
State your concerns and launch an investigative procedure immediately? *Why?*

Would you …
Launch investigative procedures? What do you need to find out?

If the rumours proved to be totally unfounded … *what would your course of action be?*

If the rumours that the woman was a prostitute proved to be unfounded … *what would you do?*

Are there additional crucial points in the process – what are the decisions or questions that might arise from them?

3   Sex for goods

Josie is an adolescent girl in one of the camps. Samuel, one of the food-distribution staff employed by Oxfam GB, has offered to give her a little extra food during distributions if she will be his 'special friend'. She agrees willingly. They agree to start a sexual relationship and neither of them thinks there is anything wrong. Josie hopes that the relationship will be a passport to a new life out of the camp. Samuel does nothing to discourage these hopes.

Who is in the right? Who is in the wrong? As Samuel's manager, what actions would you take? What broader actions you could you take to reduce the likelihood of this happening again?

4   Challenging the behaviour of colleagues

You begin a 6-month contract as Project Manager in an emergency programme. This small country has suffered more than 10 years of violent civil war, with 100,000 killed and up to 50 per cent of the remaining population displaced, their livelihoods shattered. Around 74 per cent of households are dependent on food aid.

On your first night you find a very 'macho' atmosphere among colleagues (both female and male). With little to do after work, they spend their evenings drinking beer and telling stories of threats to security on this and other assignments. Your male colleagues speak knowledgeably about gender issues and they always ensure that gender equality is considered when drawing up programme planning proposals. However, you are uncomfortable about their behaviour when dealing with female colleagues, particularly junior members of staff. It's hard to define what exactly bothers you, but when you try to raise the issue with the men, they are dismissive and patronising. As the evening wears on, someone tells an offensive, sexist joke, followed by a quick apology directed at you and a request not to 'take me too seriously'.

The working and living atmosphere is very 'closed'. There is no peaceful solution for the conflict in sight, and aid agencies operate emergency programmes in shelter, food distribution, and health care. Operations are confined to certain areas of the country (mainly close to the capital city) deemed safe enough to work; this changes on an almost daily basis as security concerns dictate.

It is an extremely stressful working environment, with high burnout and turnover of staff. All expatriate and senior local staff (15 people in all, mostly male) live together in secure accommodation close to the office in the capital city. Due to insecurity, fields trips are short. Overnight stays outside the city have been judged to be unsafe by the UN/NGO security group. A curfew operates between 6pm and 7am.

What do you do in this situation?
What are the issues you need to consider for the future?

5   Sex with young girls

Country X experienced a brutal conflict in the early 1990s, with warlords battling over the country's rich resource base until the last one was left standing. At the time of your visit, a tentative peace agreement is in place, but the capital remains tense and full of displaced people. It is a deeply impoverished and desperate existence for many.

There is a bar close to the office that is deemed safe to visit, and many international staff meet there in the evening. You go there with colleagues and are surprised to see a lot of young girls (about 12 years old) hanging around. One of your colleagues tells you that they are prostitutes, many from rural areas with no means of income, and often without family support, driven to prostitution. But apparently the real reason that girls so young are 'in demand' in preference to older women is the local belief that if a man sleeps with a young girl he has no chance of contracting HIV.

Later you are shocked to see an international staff member of another reputable INGO leaving with one of the young girls in his car. The Country Representative of the organisation in question is distressed about this and asks for advice from other agencies.

What should you have done after witnessing this act?
What should that manager do with the staff member concerned?
Are there other measures that the head of this, and other, INGOs should take in contexts such as this?

Would there be any difference in the tone and content of your discussions and decisions if the staff member who is exploiting local, underage children is himself a member of the local community?

6   Local driver

Joey is a locally hired driver working for Oxfam GB. He transports relief items from the warehouse to camps where they are distributed. On one of his trips he recognises a 15-year-old girl walking along the side of the road and gives her a lift back to the camp. Since then, to impress her and win her over, he frequently offers to drive her wherever she is going and sometimes gives her small items from the relief packages in his truck, which he thinks that she and her family could use. The last time he drove her home, she invited him inside the house to meet her family.
The family was pleased that she had made friends with an NGO worker. Joey really likes the girl and wants to start a relationship with her. He knows her family will approve.

What is Joey doing wrong?
What might the consequences of his actions be?
What would you do if you were Joey's line manager?

7   Sleeping in the camp

Staff working on a fast-paced, first-phase emergency response programme are travelling at least 4 hours a day to reach the camps in which they are delivering an integrated water and sanitation programme. They feel that the travelling is reducing their effectiveness to an unacceptable level. Their programme co-ordinator, based several hundred kilometres away in the provincial capital, receives a formal request from the team to move their living quarters from the small and inhospitable town where they currently live to the largest, and most central, of the refugee camps. This, they feel, will make them safer, less tired, and far more effective in their jobs.

If you were the programme coordinator, what would your response and your actions be?

Handout 4: Feedback form

Name (optional): _____ **Date:** _____

For each question where there is a scale, please circle the relevant number.

1. This course came at the most useful time for me to learn the maximum

Strongly   Strongly
Disagree   Agree

0   1   2   3   4   5

2. The materials and exercises were appropriate for my needs

Strongly   Strongly
Disagree   Agree

0   1   2   3   4   5

3. I have a strong sense of what I will do differently in the future

Strongly   Strongly
Disagree   Agree

0   1   2   3   4   5

4. Having to do some preparatory work before the course is a good idea that made me think about the course content before attending.

Strongly   Strongly
Disagree   Agree

0   1   2   3   4   5

Is there anything that could be done differently to raise any of the scores you have given?

How could the facilitator improve his/her skills in helping others to learn?

Flipchart 1a

Objectives of this course
As a result of this workshop,
participants will know more about
Oxfam's internal code of conduct for staff
and be better able to comply with it.

Managers will feel more confident to use the code,
and staff will understand the responsibilities
that it implies and demands.

Flipchart 1b

Objectives of this course (continued)

As a result of this workshop, we will:

Know ...

the principles that underpin Oxfam GB's Code of Conduct and the Guidelines for Sexual Conduct

Feel

confident to make judgements and decisions on the sensitive and difficult subject of sexual exploitation and abuse.

Do ...

Study cases of sexual exploitation and abuse in order to see where decisions needed to be taken and, in some cases, how they could have been improved.

Reflect on personal cases; discuss and analyse them to identify important issues, decisions, and judgements, and write these up for further use.

Flipchart 2

Rules from Oxfam's Code of Conduct

No sex with anyone under 18.

No commercial or transactional sex
with beneficiaries.

Flipchart 3

Responsibilities laid down in Oxfam's Code of Conduct

It is your duty and responsibility to report,
via the systems that exist,
behaviour that you feel is not in accordance
with the rules shown on Flipchart 2.

It is also your responsibility to actively promote
and maintain an environment
in which staff feel that they can fulfil
the organisation's expectations of them.

Flipchart 4a

Agenda for the full-day course

Introduction

Story telling

Quiz

Presentation

BREAK

Exercise 1: Oxfam GB Code of Conduct

Exercise 2: Oxfam GB Sexual Conduct Guidelines

Brainstorm: Vulnerable beneficiaries

LUNCH

Checking on the objectives

Case studies

Story telling in groups

BREAK

Group work on chosen stories

Evaluation

Review and summary

Flipchart 4b

Agenda for the half-day course

Introductions
Quiz
Presentation
Exercise 1: Oxfam GB's Code of Conduct
Exercise 2: Oxfam GB's Sexual Conduct Guidelines
BREAK
Case studies
Evaluation

Flipchart 5

Parking:
questions that will be answered later

Flipchart 6

Confidentiality

We are discussing and sharing sensitive information.
We must all respect the confidentiality of colleagues
and programmes.

No names of people or programmes will be used
during our discussions.

Failure to respect the confidences of others
during or after this course
will be considered a disciplinary offence.

If you have information that you wish to share
concerning a colleague's behaviour,
you should talk to your manager,
or your manager's manager,
or your nearest Human Resources team.

Flipchart 7

Exercise – Oxfam's Code of Conduct

You have 30 minutes for this exercise.

1 Read pages 3 and 4 of Handout 1.

2 With the person next to you,
find ...
three things that the Code definitely forbids
and three things on which you feel the Code needs
more clarity

3 Write them down for feedback to the group.

Flipchart 8

Exercise – Oxfam Guidelines on Sexual Conduct

You have 20 minutes for this exercise.

Form groups of 5 or 6.

Read Handout 2 carefully and discuss it with your group.

After 10 minutes, go to Flipcharts 8a, 8b, 8c, 8d, and 8e and add the comments of your group.

Sit down only when you have commented on ALL the questions.

Flipchart 8a

Are these guidelines exactly what you expected from Oxfam?

Did anything surprise you?

Flipchart 8b

What will be the most difficult part of the guidelines for you to implement as managers?

Flipchart 8c

Have you had to deal with staff behaviour
that breaks these rules?

Do you know of other managers
who have had to do this?

Flipchart 8d

Do you feel confident
that Oxfam would support you
if you had to deal with staff
who break these rules?

Flipchart 8e

If you could add one more rule,
what would it be?

Flipchart 9

Vulnerable beneficiaries

You have 20 minutes for this exercise.

Write down any particular features
of your region /country/ project (as appropriate)
that make beneficiaries vulnerable to abuse.

Flipchart 10

Case Studies

You have 40 minutes for this exercise.

Your group will be assigned two case studies.

Consider them carefully and answer the questions that they pose.

Write the answers down, ready to share them when all the groups have completed the exercise.

If you finish before the 40 minutes have elapsed, you may continue with any other case study, as you wish.

Flipchart 11

Evaluation

You have 10 minutes for this exercise.

Take plenty of Post-it notes and a pen with you.

Get up and walk around the room,
looking at flipcharts 11a – 11g.

Stick a Post-it note with a comment on it
on the line under each question,
in the place that best reflects how you feel
about the question.

Sit down only when you have answered
all seven questions.

Flipchart 11a

Do you think that you now know enough
about what Oxfam GB
expects from you in terms of sexual conduct?

NO .... YES

Flipchart 11b

As a manager, would you feel confident
to investigate a complaint
about inappropriate sexual behaviour?

NO .... YES

Flipchart 11c

How confident do you feel that Oxfam GB
is committed and able
to address cases of sexual misconduct?

NOT AT ALL …………………………………….VERY

Flipchart 11d

How well do you think the
'Guidelines on Sexual Conduct'
help you to regulate your behaviour
and that of those around you?

NOT WELL ……………………………….. VERY WELL

Flipchart 11e

How well do you think the
'Guidelines on Sexual Conduct'
help you to understand your own responsibilities
while working in this sector?

NOT WELL …………………………………..VERY WELL

Flipchart 11f

How capable do you feel of explaining
Oxfam GB's policy on sexual exploitation
and abuse to people with whom you work?

NOT AT ALL…………………………………….VERY

Flipchart 11g

How capable do you feel of taking responsibility
for creating and maintaining a climate
which can uphold Oxfam's
'Guidelines on Sexual Conduct'?

NOT AT ALL ....VERY

Supplementary material (1)
Preparatory text for participants

To: Participants in training session on Prevention of Sexual Exploitation and Abuse –on
       ... _facilitator to add appropriate date here_
Fm: The Facilitator
Re: Preparatory work, compulsory, for attending the training session

You will be participating in a workshop which will train you to prevent sexual exploitation and abuse within the teams and sectors in which you work. In order for you and Oxfam to gain as much value as possible from this workshop, you need to do a small amount of preparatory work. Start by reading the following information and advice carefully, to ensure that your participation is as useful as we would all like it to be.

Confidentiality
During the workshop you will be thinking and talking about behaviour that is sometimes illegal and often contravenes Oxfam GB policy. It is possible that this behaviour could be linked to colleagues, past or present, or acquaintances known to many people. It is essential that you act, within this seminar and outside it, with the utmost discretion.

In your preparatory work and in your discussions during the training session, you are forbidden to mention the name of anyone or attribute behaviour (good, bad, or otherwise) to any named individual. In addition, when describing situations, you must avoid mentioning the name of a country or location. We insist that you take these precautions to protect people's reputations and identities. Failure to do this, either within the training session or outside it, will result in disciplinary procedures being taken against you. We are very serious about this: please do your utmost to ensure that you fulfil our expectations of you.

Preparatory work
At the training session you will be asked to describe to a small group of people at least one example of sexually exploitative or abusive behaviour that you have seen in your work or everyday life, whether might either be a 'minor' or a major incident. Choose an example that you can explain clearly and on which you have an opinion.

Write down the experience, mentioning the things that seemed wrong to you, and the things that managers or others could or should have done to stop or prevent it happening.

Try to limit your story to two or three paragraphs maximum. Bring it with you to the training session. You will need this in order to participate fully, so please do write it and remember to bring it with you. If you have problems finding an example, ask your closest Human Resources person or your line manager to help you to think of something appropriate. Do not worry: everybody has at least one example to share, but it may take a bit of time to find it in your memory.

When writing down your example, please observe the guidelines given above about confidentiality: do not mention any people or places by name.

In Oxfam workshops, the facilitator will collect the examples that participants bring with them, so that they can be added to the pool of information, case studies, and examples that we (and our partners eventually) can use to learn and improve our performance.

Thank you. I look forward to seeing you at our training session.

Supplementary information (2)
Sample stories
(Not a handout: intended for facilitator's use only)

Example 1

Ignatius is a middle-ranking civil servant in country X who has been posted from the capital city to the far northern district, where he has been assigned to supervise government registration of the refugees who have come *en masse*, fleeing conflict over the border.

The refugees, many of whom are women separated from their male relatives, are extremely vulnerable, having been on the move for several weeks, and subject to attacks. They have arrived in a very poor area of the host country, where they find that people of their ethnic identity and religion are unwelcome.

Oxfam is setting up a humanitarian operation and relies on keeping good relations with the host government. However, staff are beginning to hear rumours that Ignatius and his colleagues are sexually exploiting refugee women. There is no direct evidence, because the alleged abuse takes place at night, when Oxfam staff are not allowed into the makeshift camps.

Example 2

An INGO was running a long-term programme in support of commercial sex workers in a country that had been wracked by an extremely violent civil war for more than two decades. The aim of the programme was to offer commercial sex workers some choices in their lives and also offer some safety and dignity while they were working.

It took a long, long time to gain the trust of the women involved. Many of them had horrific stories to tell and not much confidence in other people, not even those who really wanted to help.

Early one morning one of the sex workers was seen, by a colleague, leaving the room of the male programme co-ordinator. This colleague confronted the programme co-ordinator, who denied any impropriety.

Example 3

While on a field trip to IDP camps, an expatriate gender adviser observed that throughout the course of her meetings with camp inhabitants her driver sat in the shade and chatted with young women, presumably residents of the camp.

On the journey home she asked the driver what he had been talking about with the women. The driver took offence and said that nothing bad had been going on. The gender adviser assured him that she had not believed that this had been the case, but she was interested in the fact that unaccompanied young women could feel at ease talking to a 'stranger'. The gender adviser then went on to explain that it was important for everybody to understand how vulnerable women in camps were – how little support or power they had, and how difficult it was to remain safe in such harsh circumstances.

On returning to base, she discussed this with some of her expatriate colleagues. Some of the male field-workers told her that she didn't know what it was like to work in the camps. "The women come up to us all the time, offering to be our girlfriends." "They say 'look around you, there are no men, you can be our men'. They say this all the time."

Again it took quite a lot of discussion for some colleagues to realise how vulnerable women and children were in the camps, how much they needed ,and what this might push them to do. The gender adviser has the impression that this might be the first time some of her colleagues have really thought about this situation from the point of view of the women in the camps.

Example 4

The wife of an accompanied staff member made complaints that two colleagues were bringing prostitutes to an NGO compound where she, her family, and the two colleagues lived.

The Head of Mission, after taking advice from Human Resources, spoke informally with both men. She emphasised that their actions, although not forbidden by their NGO's Internal Code of Conduct, caused distress to the family of a colleague, and risked bringing Oxfam into disrepute. She emphasised that further complaints would necessitate formal disciplinary action.

The staff members continued to use prostitutes, but discreetly, and not on the NGO's property. Senior staff members checked regularly with the family who had raised the complaint, to ensure that their concerns had been resolved.

Example 5

An expatriate male manager of a small programme team lived alone in a big house in the town in which his NGO had an office and some programmes. He was well known in town, because there were few expatriates living there, and fewer still 'aid' cars.

On several occasions, other staff visited the programme, staying overnight in the programme manager's house. Sometimes when staff stayed there, he would come home very late, often quite drunk and occasionally with a 'girlfriend'. Only when several staff members had the occasion to meet did they compare their stories of staying in the programme manager's house and then they realised the extent of the problem. Putting all the stories together, it seemed that the programme manager was going out drinking three or four nights a week, and on most of those occasions he brought home a different girl.

Still nothing was done about trying to curb or regulate this behaviour; he was not even challenged on it. The issue did not come to a head until one of the visiting senior members of staff was approached by someone in the street one day with a written request to mend a garden wall that had been allegedly knocked down by the manager while he was driving home drunk.

It was decided that, as the programme manager had only two more months until the end of his contract, he should not be dismissed, but he should not be offered an extension. Nothing was said about his drinking or his sleeping with so many local girls.

Example 6

During a recruitment process, an NGO was about to recruit an extremely well-qualified and experienced expatriate Programme Manager. However, the Country Head of Mission had heard rumours in the region about this Programme Manager's personal behaviour: reportedly he was using prostitutes and drinking heavily. There was no evidence of this at the interview, however, and when the question of his conduct was raised with the candidate, he said that he was aware of the NGO's policy and he assured the Head of Mission that he was happy to abide by it. Reassured, the Head of Mission chose to appoint him.

Three months after the Programme Manager took up his post, rumours reached the Country Office of an inappropriate relationship between him and a junior female member of staff, thirty years younger than he was. Upon discreet investigation, two guards asserted that the female staff member had stayed overnight at the Programme Manager's house on at least one occasion. Three staff asserted that the relationship was common knowledge; a number of other field staff refused to comment.

The Head of Mission and their Deputy went on a field visit, during which the Head of Mission witnessed the Programme Manager attempt to kiss the junior staff member, who resisted him. It was also noted that the junior staff member had a very high rate of sick leave. Both the Head of Mission and the Deputy verbally reasserted the NGO's policy on line–staff relationships to the Programme Manager. (An appropriate Internal Code of Conduct had not then been introduced.)

The Head of Mission asked the advice of his line manager, and was told that such behaviour was unacceptable and should be addressed. Rumours of the relationship continued to circulate among national staff. When the Programme Manager passed through the Country Office prior to his Rest & Recuperation break, he and the Head of Mission met together to review the probationary period. The Head of Mission asked about the rumours, which the Programme Manager denied, asserting that the relationship was just a close friendship. The Head of Mission chose not to confirm the Programme Manager in post, and he was asked not to return after his R&R. The grounds for non-confirmation were 'incompatible beliefs'.

When he reached the UK, the Programme Manager raised his concerns about his treatment with a number of senior managers. There was no witness to his meeting with the Head of Mission, and the case and process had been poorly documented. The Programme Manager threatened to take the NGO to an employment tribunal for wrongful dismissal, and threatened to sue for defamation of character.

Senior managers in the NGO agreed to give the Programme Manager a good reference, in return for an agreement not to take his legal actions further. They also paid for him to make a return visit to the country, and to his field office. They did not ask for written statements from any of the programme staff or management involved, or speak to any in-country staff involved, apart from the Head of Mission. The line manager of the Head of Mission supported the decision.

After a period of some months, the Programme Manager was re-employed in another programme run by the NGO. The sickness record of the junior member of staff involved improved significantly following the departure of the Programme Manager.

Example 7

Aid-workers in a remote small town in central Africa have limited access to other expatriates, do not speak local languages well, and are in desperate need of more social interaction! The arrival of small numbers of peace-keepers creates great excitement. They welcome the UN blue-berets happily and arrange a couple of evenings of entertainment at their respective homes before venturing out into town together.

This all seems like nice, innocent fun – but what might the repercussions be?

Supplementary information (3)
'Answers' to Case Studies described in Handout 3
(Not a handout – intended for facilitator's use only)

1 Use of Oxfam laptop to access pornographic websites

1a   First scenario
From Oxfam GB's Internet Use Policy:

'The following are some examples of misuse which would be classified as acts of gross misconduct under the disciplinary procedures and as such may result in summary dismissal, without prior warning and notice. The list is not exhaustive:

- violating the privacy of other users;

- corrupting or destroy other users' data or disrupting their work;

- creating, accessing or displaying any criminal, offensive, obscene or indecent images, data or other material.'

Therefore this is an act that deserves sanction through the disciplinary procedures. The staff member has broken the terms of his contract and has not followed Oxfam GB's procedures, instructions, and policy as set out in the Internet Use Policy. Decisions about what sanction(s) to apply are left to the line manager, but it is clear that, if he remains with Oxfam, at the very least his ability to abide by Oxfam's Internal Code of Conduct will become a Performance Management issue.

There have been cases of immediate dismissal for gross misconduct of staff members who access pornographic websites.

In addition to dealing with the staff member concerned, the manager(s) should take the opportunity of a staff meeting to remind staff about the Internal Code and the guidance on Sexual Conduct. For further training, they should consider using case studies appropriate to the context.

1b   Second scenario
This, for the staff member committing the 'Oxfam crime', is still a disciplinary offence, because the policy above states that this is so. The offending staff member probably deserves a formal, verbal warning with a note in his file to record that this has been done. In addition, the staff member's manager, for failing to ensure that the code of conduct was given to the employee, should be held responsible for this transgression and should probably receive a formal, verbal warning also. The manager's failure to conduct an adequate induction should become a performance-management issue.

The staff member must, immediately, be given a copy of the Code of Conduct and should be given training to understand the responsibility that the Code requires. The staff member's manager must be made very aware of his or her responsibility to promote and maintain an atmosphere in which staff can and will observe Oxfam's guidelines and rulings on sexual abuse and exploitation and sexual conduct. Employees' willingness and ability to do this is a performance-management issue and should be closely monitored.

Every effort must be made to reinforce key messages about Oxfam's rules on the use of equipment, and the responsibility of all to promote and maintain conditions in which staff can and will uphold the Internal Code.

1c   Third scenario

As with the answer given above, a formal, verbal warning would probably be the most appropriate primary response – both for the staff member concerned and for the manager (with notes added to their files to record that this has been done). However, in addition, it is obvious that some work needs to be done with the staff member to help him to understand, and live up to, Oxfam GB's Internal Code of Conduct and guidelines for sexual conduct.

It must be clear to all staff, whatever their level, that Oxfam GB is fully aware that the global culture that we are promoting is sometimes not in accordance with local culture. On this issue, in all circumstances, Oxfam GB culture should override local culture – always.

It would probably be a good idea to conduct training/reminder sessions with all staff at an opportune moment. The judgements made by Oxfam GB on what is acceptable behaviour and what is not may differ, quite radically, from a local 'norm'. Although these differences are interesting, and much can be learned from debating them, <u>the fundamental point is that Oxfam GB has thought long and hard about these issues and has prescribed rules and guidelines that it feels are necessary and appropriate</u>. Staff members must be able and willing to promote and maintain these rules and guidelines; if not, they, and their managers, should recognise that they are working for the wrong organisation, and they need to leave.

2   Personal relationships

One or two whispers of the same rumour should be quite enough for the manager of this Programme Co-ordinator (PC) to act. This is for two reasons: (a) prostitution is illegal in country X, so the PC is breaking the law; and (b) sleeping with a prostitute, in this given situation, shows extremely poor judgement, because of the inevitably negative effect on Oxfam's reputation.

(Managers should note that if they hear even one rumour that sexual activity is taking place with children – i.e. anybody under the age of 18 – then <u>they must act immediately</u>. It is not necessary to wait for two or three more rumours to come trickling in.)

In this case the actions constitute misconduct according to Oxfam's Code of Conduct, which commits every member of staff to the following obligations:

> **'Avoid involvement in any criminal activities**, activities that contravene human rights or those that compromise the work of Oxfam GB.

> **Contribute to combating all forms of illegal activities.**

> **Seek to ensure that my sexual conduct does not bring Oxfam GB into any ill repute** and does not impact on or undermine my ability to undertake the role for which I am employed.'

So in this case, as soon as the manager is reasonably sure that this is a case of misconduct, he or she must travel to the area where the Programme Co-ordinator works and confront him with the rumours. In addition the manager might consider whether to suspend him pending investigation. Suspension, it must be made clear, implies no judgement about the truth of the allegations. Suspension is necessary in order to remove the person (or people) most involved from the immediate vicinity, in order to protect them while an investigation takes place.

It is important, from the very beginning, to keep a written record of what is said and what is done.

If the Programme Co-ordinator denies the rumours and there is evidence to support him, then life can return to normal. But the manager needs to find the source of the rumours and investigate why they started and, very importantly, what needs to be done to rebuild team spirit, cohesion, and confidence.

If the PC admits that the rumours are true, the recommended course of action would be to dismiss him immediately and ask him to leave the programme without delay. It would probably be difficult to find an interim replacement for him, but not sacking him would demonstrate to staff and others that Oxfam GB lacks the conviction to act on its internal guiding principles; and that would set a very bad example.

If he denies the rumours but there is evidence to support them, the manager has a big problem. The precise response to it will depend on the particular context, and it is difficult to prescribe the correct course of action without further information. The manager could initiate an investigation, but should be aware that investigative procedures are lengthy and costly in time, energy, and resources – to such an extent that they are often not cost-effective. It is probably best in these circumstances for the manager to inform the PC that he is not believed, and for what reasons. The PC needs to know that the manager (and colleagues in the PC's team) no longer trust his judgement and leadership, and that it will be very difficult to make the management relationship work again.

A formal investigation, however, can sometimes be a useful way to establish the facts and clear the air. If one needs to check the veracity of the rumours, it is important that ONLY first-hand evidence is considered. Hearsay, or reporting what someone else might have said or might have seen, is not good enough and not admissible.

Making decisions like this is not easy, but managers should remember that they can, and must, request support whenever they feel the need for it.

It is important to realise that, whether it is true or not, this 'story' has damaged staff morale and trust, and work will be needed to repair the damage. In addition the Code of Conduct needs to be reintroduced, to ensure that it is known, understood, and used as a management tool in the future.

If trust within the team has completely broken down, it may be necessary to move the PC out of his present job. It may also be necessary to deal with any staff members who were responsible for spreading malicious rumours.

3   Sex for goods

Samuel is exploiting Josie and abusing Oxfam property for his own personal benefit. Josie is a beneficiary and she has the right to expect that Oxfam staff will exercise their full duty of care for her. In addition, Samuel is stealing from Oxfam. These are both acts of gross misconduct, in contravention of Oxfam's Code of Conduct, and Samuel should expect to be dismissed.

4   Challenging the behaviour of colleagues

There are no easy right answers to this question, because there are many complicated things going on. Ideally one would talk, either in public or in private, to the staff member who had made the offensive, sexist joke and try to get him or her to understand that Oxfam GB does not tolerate this type of behaviour.

In addition, sessions could be held to reinforce general awareness of the organisation's Anti-Harassment Policy, the Code of Conduct, and the Gender Policy. It would probably be best to deal with this problem as a team.
Attention should probably also be paid to the policy on Rest and Recuperation and, over time, to the gender balance of the team.

Continued behaviour of the kind described in the case study must be considered as harassment, and any staff member concerned has the right and the responsibility to bring grievance or disciplinary procedures against the offending staff member, as appropriate.

5   Sex with young girls

The Oxfam GB staff member who witnessed this act should have written to the in-country head of the NGO concerned, describing exactly what he had witnessed. The letter should have been copied to the in-country head of his own agency.

The Oxfam staff member is responsible only for reporting what he witnessed. The most senior Oxfam GB manager in the location is **duty-bound** to ensure that the incident is considered and addressed by the senior manager of the 'accused' organisation. Our legal obligations in terms of the actions of other organisations are very few; but if one member of an organisation is doing something very wrong, we all have a duty to inform a senior manager, in order that the case can be dealt with.

In future one will also be able to report such a concern to *'focal points' for sexual exploitation and abuse*. These agency staff will form networks and meet regularly with each other to discuss relevant issues, and they will advise agency heads on policy and practice.

In this case, the manager of the staff member concerned should consider, first, the health and safety of the young girl. If the 'offending' staff member admits that he has slept with her, or if he denies it but his manager does not believe him, every effort must be made to ensure that the girl has access to all appropriate support services.

This is clearly an allegation of gross misconduct. The staff member should be suspended until the facts of the case are established to the senior manager's satisfaction. If it is proved that the staff member has been sleeping with a girl who is under age (defined as 'under the age of 18' in UN guidelines and the Convention on the Rights of the Child), he should be summarily dismissed. If the allegations remain unproved, the senior manager should probably encourage the staff member involved to move on to another job.

If a senior manager does decides that it is necessary to move a staff member to a new job (or encourages him or her to leave the organisation), it is essential that they should discuss and agree the matter between them. Under no circumstances should the relationship break down to such an extent that it is impossible to have such a discussion. Managers who do not discuss, honestly, the reasons why they have lost confidence in a staff member or feel they that the staff member is no longer the best person to do the job are failing in their responsibility to their organisation.

It is a manager's responsibility to ensure that staff know the Code of Conduct and any related policies that regulate staff behaviour, and that they fully understand the implications for their behaviour – both in terms of what they do, personally, and what they are responsible for (creating and maintaining an environment in which the Code is understood and adhered to).

6   Local driver

Joey is in the wrong, already, for several reasons:

- He should not give lifts to somebody who is not a member of staff and who is not authorised to travel in an Oxfam vehicle. A stern warning, if not disciplinary procedure, is appropriate.
- He should not be giving her 'gifts' that are not his to give, even if he has asked for nothing in return. A stern warning, if not disciplinary procedure, is appropriate.
- If he starts a relationship with her, he will be guilty of exploitation – both for sleeping with an under-age girl and for exchanging goods for sexual favours. It will be classed as gross misconduct, and formal disciplinary procedures will be immediately started. Joey will be suspended from work until the case is proved or disproved. If it is proved, he will immediately lose his job.

In all likelihood, many managers would feel the need (and under most circumstances would be advised) to dismiss Joey (with due process) for giving unauthorised lifts and gifts to a beneficiary, even without proof of a sexual relationship.

7   Sleeping in the camp

The manager should immediately and firmly refuse to allow staff to stay overnight in the camps. This is for a number of reasons. To name but a few:

- Conditions in the camp are likely to be very dangerous for aid workers, with little chance of improving the standards of security.
- As aid workers living in the camp, they would get no peace whatsoever. They would constantly receive requests for support and assistance and would find it almost impossible to protect themselves against this.
- They would inevitably become a target for those seeking a way out of the camp. Offers of sexual favours would become difficult to ignore, and behaving in the fair and transparent way that Oxfam GB expects would become increasingly difficult.
- There is certain to be a high level of HIV infection among the camp population, and any sexual activity would expose staff to severe risks.
- The presence of relatively high-earning aid workers with seemingly endless resources would create jealousy and poor perceptions of the workers and/or organisation involved, which may well lead to difficulties in programme implementation.

Supplementary information (4)
Frequently asked questions: some thoughts

(Not a handout: intended for facilitator's use only)

'But in my country the age of consent is lower than 18 and it is culturally acceptable to marry girls as young as 15.'
In many countries this **is** the case. Some staff feel that setting our age limit higher is inappropriate and will be too difficult to implement. But the facilitator should point out that nearly all international NGOs accept the terms of the UN Convention on the Rights of the Child (to which virtually all countries are signatory), which enshrines the principle that childhood should defined as continuing up to the age of 18.

'My colleague X has been married for the last two years to somebody who is now only 17. Are you going to fire him?'
It is unlikely that this will be legally possible. But, now that Oxfam GB has adopted 18 as the age of consent, we will not tolerate any member of staff, whether newly appointed or long-established, starting a relationship with a child. When recruiting new staff in some countries, we will be able to ask about marital status at interview. In others this will not be legally permissible, but we will make every effort to find out the information. Our recruitment procedures will be much more robust, to enable us to offer maximum protection to people in our care. When advertising vacancies, we will make very clear our position on the protection of children. And then we will rigorously follow up candidates' references and investigate their employment history and criminal records where possible. In addition we will increase the level of attention that we pay to these issues in our day-to-day work, and managers and staff alike will be more confident and competent to make our working environment safe for vulnerable people.

'Prostitution is legal in this country. Many people pay for sex with sex workers. There is little stigma attached to it.'
Yes, we know. We are not banning the use of sex workers, but we are **strongly** recommending people to avoid using them – for many reasons. First of all there is the fundamental principle that any transaction of this sort is the result of an unequal balance of power and is therefore exploitative. There is every possibility that indulging in transactional sex will bring the organisation into disrepute, and there is often the distinct possibility that it will increase security risks for individuals and Oxfam alike. There is also every chance that it will have direct security implications for the sex workers themselves.

'If Oxfam takes such a strong stance on gender equity, why hasn't it banned the use of sex workers? I would feel much happier if it did.'
No, we haven't banned the use of prostitutes, but we **strongly** discourage it. We don't ban it, because we cannot infringe on people's civil liberties, and we know it would be impractical to try to enforce a total ban. Also, in a number of countries we support partner organisations that support sex workers to claim their basic rights; we are definitely not in any position to tell sex workers how to live their lives.

'You might think that my relationship is exploitative, but it doesn't feel like that to me, or to my partner. You are not in a position to pass judgement.'
This might be true. But if this relationship involves a minor or a beneficiary, then our fundamental principles tell us that this situation is, by its very nature, exploitative and is not something that Oxfam will condone … indeed, disciplinary action can and should result immediately.

If the relationship does not involve a minor or a beneficiary, there is less justification for Oxfam GB to intervene or pass judgement. But f you, as a manager, feel that there is something exploitative about the relationship, then you are probably right. Therefore it is worth investigating.

'If we are so keen to protect children, why do we not have tighter checks on people as they enter the organisation?'
We appreciate the need for this, and we work to improve our procedures is already underway. We are taking advice from other specialist agencies in the field, and the new procedures that we draw up will reflect our absolute duty of care to those in our charge, and also the need for greater resources in order to implement more robust procedures.

'Yes, I am having a relationship with a beneficiary, but I haven't given anything in exchange, so I am not exploiting the power that I have or the position that I hold within the organisation.'
Maybe not. But others will probably not either see or appreciate this fact. So, in order to avoid any damage to Oxfam GB's reputation, sexual relationships with beneficiaries are forbidden. We need to guard ourselves and our beneficiaries against the *potential* for abuse, as well as the abuse itself.

'I know many Oxfam GB staff who are having relationships within their management line. What does Oxfam feel about this, and what guidance can it offer to me, or others, if we find ourselves in this situation?'
Oxfam GB does not forbid relationships within the management line, but it does insist on transparency. If you are having a relationship with somebody whom you manage, it is **your** responsibility to inform **your** manager. It is then up to the manager (and maybe others) to decide whether the relationship could result in a potential conflict of interest. In all such cases it is not acceptable for one partner to manage the performance of another, and Oxfam GB would need to find an alternative procedure.

'The Oxfam Code is vague about sexual conduct and is not prescriptive enough to help managers.'
It is not so much vague as rather broad. In addition, we don't yet have a policy on sexual conduct, so we can't refer you to it for further clarity and guidance. What we do have are the 'Sexual Conduct Guidelines', and this training pack; and soon Sexual Exploitation Focal Points will be appointed in each region and project area, as appropriate. Meanwhile Oxfam staff should feel free to contact Yo Winder (ywinder@oxfam.org.uk) or Justine Tordoff (jtordoff@oxfam.org.uk) and/or their closest Human Resources team for further guidance.

Quick Quiz – PPT1

Power imbalance / risks / what to do?

PICK–UP–AND–GO

What is in the Code of Conduct?

- A brief summary of behaviour that Oxfam GB expects from staff.

- A list of all the other policies that you should read or know about.

- Your signature to show that you know what is in the Code and that you understand it and will do what it says.

- Rules on the sexual conduct that Oxfam GB expects from staff.

PICK–UP–AND–GO

To whom does the Oxfam GB Code of Conduct apply?

- All Oxfam GB staff members and volunteers in the whole world.

Slide 3

PICK–UP–AND–GO

Does Oxfam GB tolerate abuse of power?

- No

- There will always be those who have more 'power' than others. But this power should not be abused. In particular it should not be used to make people do things that go against Oxfam's values and beliefs.

PICK–UP–AND–GO

Slide 5

What is power?

- Force
- Influence
- Strength
- Pressure
- ?

PICK–UP–AND–GO

Who holds power?

- Men or women
- Driver or manager
- Adult or child
- Beneficiary or government official
- Military or civilian
- Beneficiary or relief worker

Slide 6

PICK–UP–AND–GO

What is power imbalance?

- When one person has a lot more leverage or opportunity to make another person do something.

- Result?

- The ability to make a person feel that he or she must do or believe what another person says.

- The ability to make somebody do something that they do not want to do or know to be wrong.

PICK–UP–AND–GO

How does Oxfam GB try to ensure that power is not abused?

- Oxfam GB's internal Staff Code of Conduct.

- Oxfam GB 'whistle-blowing' policy.

- (What is whistle-blowing?)

- The action of reporting, correctly, behaviour of a colleague that in your view breaks Oxfam GB policy or that you find offensive.

- Performance Management process.

PICK–UP–AND–GO

Which particular abuses of power cause Oxfam GB the greatest concern?

- Staff behaviour towards other staff.

- Staff behaviour towards beneficiaries.

Slide 9

PICK–UP–AND–GO

Presentation – PPT2

Prevention of sexual abuse and exploitation of beneficiaries by Oxfam GB staff

Slide 1

PICK–UP–AND–GO

Incidents of sexual exploitation and abuse

- Liberia, Sierra Leone, Guinea in 2001
- Nepal in 2001
- Democratic Republic of Congo in 2003
- By relief/aid workers, sometimes by Oxfam staff
- Oxfam has dismissed staff for exploiting or abusing beneficiaries or members of the local community in virtually every recent humanitarian response.

Slide 2

PICK–UP–AND–GO

Why does sexual exploitation and abuse of beneficiaries happen?

- Because of the imbalance of power between aid workers and beneficiaries.

- Because beneficiaries need resources to survive.

- Because it comes to be thought of as 'normal'.

Slide 3

PICK–UP–AND–GO

Why is Oxfam concerned to prevent exploitation and abuse of beneficiaries of humanitarian programmes?

Because

- we know there is a huge imbalance of power

- it is gross dereliction of our 'duty of care' to our beneficiaries

- it affects those who are already most vulnerable

Slide 4

PICK–UP–AND–GO

What would be the consequences for an organisation whose staff committed this type of offence?

Very bad for

- its reputation
- its programmes
- its funding
- its faith in itself

- In fact, it is very bad for the **relief community in general,** for all the reasons stated above.

Slide 5

PICK–UP–AND–GO

So what has Oxfam GB done to reduce the risk of staff committing acts of exploitation and abuse?

• Strong leadership and clear communication from the Director.

• The Code of Conduct has become part of the contract and induction process.

• Responsibility for ensuring adherence to the Code is clearly ascribed to line managers.

• Training packs, tools, training support are available.

• Regional Focal Points exist who 'champion' this work in addition to their normal jobs.

Slide 6

PICK–UP–AND–GO

What is expected of you as managers and leaders?

- Take responsibility for the behaviour of your staff.

- Promote and maintain an environment where staff know what behaviour you expect from them.

- Ensure that staff always act with respect towards beneficiaries and each other.

- Know what is going on in your programmes.

- Take decisions and action when necessary if behaviour or attitudes contravene the Code of Conduct.

- Ask for help as and when you need it!

PICK–UP–AND–GO

What support is available for you to prevent sexual exploitation and abuse?

- Your Human Resources team or staff member.
- Your regional/country/programme focal point.
- For Oxfam staff: the Oxfam GB intranet.
- For Oxfam staff: the staff Code of Conduct and Sexual Conduct Guidelines.
- For Oxfam staff: training packs and other tools to support the adoption of the staff Code of Conduct and Sexual Conduct Guidelines.
- Focal points in the UN or other agencies.

Slide 8

PICK–UP–AND–GO

What should the organisation think of doing next to continue its prevention work?

- Think about donors' expectations of staff behaviour?

- Think about whether it is appropriate (and how) to get partners to align with our Code of Conduct?

- Listen to managers and focal points: adapt/produce more tools/deliver more training as necessary.

- Ensure that countries/programmes at risk have nominated focal points.

Slide 9

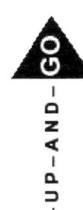

PICK–UP–AND–GO

Gender Equality and Sexual Exploitation: CD-ROM

The CD supplied with this publication contains files of all the materials that are included in the book:

- Introduction to Gender Equality
- Mainstreaming Gender Equality in NGOs
- Preventing Sexual Exploitation and Abuse

On the CD the original English-language texts are accompanied by full translations into French, Portuguese, and Spanish.

You will need Acrobat Reader to view these files. A copy is included on the CD. Please install it first by clicking on the 'Reader' icon. It may take a few minutes to install.

If you copy all the files from the CD to the hard drive of your computer, you will speed up your access to the material. Create a folder in your hard drive, and then copy all the files into that folder.

The Handout files for each module are presented in Word format, to allow them to be   pted for use in particular contexts – subject to the copyright restrictions stated   ont of this book.

Access to the external web sites included in the CD is possible only if you have an Internet connection.